Main

favourites

10 9 8 7 6 5 4 3 2 1

Published in 2013 by BBC Books, an imprint of Ebury Publishing
A Random House Group company

The Random House Group Limited
Reg. No. 954009

Addresses for companies within the Random House Group can be found at www.randomhouse.co.uk

A CIP catalogue record for this book is available from the British Library

The Random House Group Limited supports the Forest Stewardship Council® (FSC®), the leading
international forest-certification organisation. Our books carrying the FSC label are printed on FSC®-certified
paper. FSC is the only forest-certification scheme supported by the leading environmental organisations,
including Greenpeace. Our paper procurement policy can be found at www.randomhouse.co.uk/environment

To buy your favourite authors and register for offers visit www.randomhouse.co.uk

Printed and bound by Firmengruppe APPL, aprinta druck, Wemding, Germany
Colour origination by Dot Gradations Ltd, UK

Commissioning Editor: Muna Reyal
Project Editor: Lizzy Gaisford
Designer: Kathryn Gammon
Production: Rebecca Jones
Picture Researcher: Gabby Harrington

ISBN: 9781849906692

MIX
Paper from
responsible sources
FSC® C004592
www.fsc.org

Picture credits

BBC *Good Food* magazine and BBC Books would like to thank the following people for providing photos. While every effort
has been made to trace and acknowledge all photographers, we should like to apologise should there be any errors or
omissions.

Marie-Louise Avery p197; Carolyn Barber p133; Peter Cassidy p33, p47, p39, p63, p87, p127, p135, p159, p165, p187;
Jean Cazals p25, p31, p35, p181, p203; Will Heap p29, p55, p65, p81, p117, p173; Lara Holmes p109, p145; Sian Irvine p59;
Jonathan Kennedy p89; William Lingwood p103; Gareth Morgans p19, p67, p83, p97, p191; Noel Murphy p177; David Munns
p11, p15, p69, p61, p73, p75, p95, p107, p131, p137, p151, p153, p161, p179, p205, p209; Myles New p17, p37, p41, p43, p45,
p49, p51, p71, p77, p91, p167; Stuart Ovenden p13, p27, p105, p113, p121, p125, p169, p199, p207, p185; Lis Parsons p53,
p85, p139, p111, p157, p175, p155, p183, p195; Maja Smend p57; Simon Smith p143; Howard Shooter p119; Yuki Sugiura
p23, p147; Debi Treloar p21; Simon Walton p171; Philip Webb p93, p99, p101, p123, p141, p163, p189, p193, p201, p211;
Simon Wheeler p115; Elizabeth Zeschin p129

All the recipes in this book were created by the editorial team at *Good Food* and by regular contributors to BBC Magazines.

easy

GoodFood
Pressure cooker favourites

Editor **Barney Desmazery**

BBC
BOOKS

Contents

Introduction

If, like me, you grew up with a pressure cooker clanking away on the stove – things have changed. Today's pressure cookers have been redesigned and updated to become safe pans that have no chance of bursting.

I was re-enlightened to the joys of pressure-cooking on a photo shoot when a clever food stylist, stuck for time, ignored the instructions to slow-roast some ribs for 3 hours and cooked them in her new pressure cooker for just 30 minutes. The ribs were so tender you could literally slip the bones away from the meat. They were the best ribs we had ever tasted – so we all went out and bought a pressure cooker!

Since then my pressure cooker has become as essential as any other piece of kitchen kit and is perhaps the most used item too. It has changed the way I cook on weeknights, for instance; now when I'm late home and stuck for time I can make a stew, braise or casserole in under an hour, or get a risotto on the table in less than 15 minutes.

Speed isn't the only advantage of pressure-cooking, though, it is also the healthy option because it preserves nutrients and vitamins, and provides a more economical way of cooking. Yet purely on taste alone I firmly believe that there are some jobs, like cooking lentils or tough cuts of meat, that can't be done better than in a pressure cooker.

In this book we have used the pressure cooker to all its strengths with a great mix of recipes from the familiar made a lot faster to more adventurous dishes that prove that pressure-cooking doesn't mean old-fashioned food. From the freshest-tasting soups to indulgent steamed puddings cooked in a quarter of the time, this book is packed with recipes that will make you change the way you cook today.

Happy pressure-cooking !

Barney

Getting the best from your pressure cooker

Though pressure cookers all work on the same principle, make sure you read the manufacturer's instructions for your device, paying special attention to any safety points, before using it. Here we'll share with you the *Good Food* team's top tips for pressure cooking and some of the terminology we use in the following recipes.

• Pressure cookers generally cook on two levels of pressure; in this book they are referred to as low and high. All cooking times should be taken only from when the level of pressure is reached, at which point the cook should lower the heat but try to maintain the same level of pressure for the time stated – this can involve turning the heat up and down during the cooking process or moving the pan to different-sized gas rings.

• Different models will have different ways of releasing the pressure. In this book we refer to two ways: fast and slow. Fast means the fastest method given in the instruction manual and slow means just to turn off the heat and let the pressure drop naturally until it's safe to remove the lid. If a recipe says to slow-release, the food will carry on cooking as the pressure drops so it's important that this instruction is followed. Never try to force the lid of a pressure cooker open.

• As pressure cookers cook so quickly it is essential that you use a timer, because the difference of a minute or two can be the difference between a perfect or ruined dish.

• All the recipes in this book have been tested with pressure cookers that have the capacity of at least 5 litres. For smaller pressure cookers quantities may need to be pared down to fit in all the ingredients safely.

• Pressure-cooking intensifies flavours, so be aware of this when seasoning a recipe before cooking or adding salty ingredients like stock cubes.

• Always cook with at least the minimum amount of liquid stated by the manufacturer and never overfill your pressure cooker.

Notes and conversion tables

NOTES ON THE RECIPES
- Eggs are large in the UK and Australia and extra large in America unless stated.
- Wash fresh produce before preparation.
- Recipes contain nutritional analyses for 'sugar', which means the total sugar content including all natural sugars in the ingredients, unless otherwise stated.

OVEN TEMPERATURES

Gas	°C	°C Fan	°F	Oven temp.
¼	110	90	225	Very cool
½	120	100	250	Very cool
1	140	120	275	Cool or slow
2	150	130	300	Cool or slow
3	160	140	325	Warm
4	180	160	350	Moderate
5	190	170	375	Moderately hot
6	200	180	400	Fairly hot
7	220	200	425	Hot
8	230	210	450	Very hot
9	240	220	475	Very hot

APPROXIMATE WEIGHT CONVERSIONS
- All the recipes in this book list both metric and imperial measurements. Conversions are approximate and have been rounded up or down. Follow one set of measurements only; do not mix the two.
- Cup measurements, which are used by cooks in Australia and America, have not been listed here as they vary from ingredient to ingredient. Kitchen scales should be used to measure dry/solid ingredients.

Good Food are concerned about sustainable sourcing and animal welfare so where possible we use organic ingredients, humanely reared meats, sustainably caught fish, free-range chickens and eggs and unrefined sugar.

SPOON MEASURES

Spoon measurements are level unless otherwise specified.

- 1 teaspoon (tsp) = 5ml
- 1 tablespoon (tbsp) = 15ml
- 1 Australian tablespoon = 20ml (cooks in Australia should measure 3 teaspoons where 1 tablespoon is specified in a recipe)

APPROXIMATE LIQUID CONVERSIONS

metric	imperial	AUS	US
50ml	2fl oz	¼ cup	¼ cup
125ml	4fl oz	½ cup	½ cup
175ml	6fl oz	¾ cup	¾ cup
225ml	8fl oz	1 cup	1 cup
300ml	10fl oz/½ pint	½ pint	1¼ cups
450ml	16fl oz	2 cups	2 cups/1 pint
600ml	20fl oz/1 pint	1 pint	2½ cups
1 litre	35fl oz/1¾ pints	1¾ pints	1 quart

Butternut squash & sage soup

This big-batch hearty soup can also be made with pumpkin and is ideal for freezing.

TAKES 40 MINUTES ● SERVES 8

1 tbsp olive oil
1 tbsp butter
3 onions, chopped
2 tbsp chopped sage leaves
1.4kg/3lb 3oz peeled deseeded
    butternut squash
1 tbsp clear honey
1 litre/1¾ pints vegetable stock, plus
    extra to thin (optional)
bunch chives, snipped, and cracked
    black pepper, to garnish

1 Melt the oil and butter in the pressure cooker. Add the onions and sage, and gently cook, uncovered, for about 15 minutes until soft.

2 Tip in the squash and cook for 2–3 minutes, stirring. Add the honey and stock and close the lid. Bring up to high pressure and cook for 6 minutes then leave the pressure to release slowly.

3 Let the soup cool a little, then whizz until really smooth with a hand blender straight in the pressure cooker, or in batches in a food processor. Season to taste, adding a drop more stock or water if the soup is too thick. Reheat before serving, and serve sprinkled with chives and cracked black pepper.

PER SERVING 130 kcals, protein 3g, carbs 21g, fat 4g, sat fat 1g, fibre 5g, sugar 14g, salt 0.5g

Peppered potato soup

Keep this thrifty soup an attractive pale colour by using the white bottom end of the leek only.

TAKES 30 MINUTES • SERVES 4

25g/1oz butter
1 large leek, sliced and washed
few fresh thyme sprigs, 3 bay leaves
    and parsley stalks tied into a bundle
2 medium floury potatoes, chopped
    into walnut-sized chunks
850ml/1½ pints chicken or vegetable
    stock
3 tbsp double cream
chopped parsley leaves, to garnish
crusty bread, to serve

1 Heat the butter in a pressure cooker until sizzling then add the leek and herbs, and cook gently for 5 minutes until soft. Stir the potatoes into the leeks and season with a little salt and lots of freshly ground pepper.

2 Pour over the stock, close the lid, bring up to high pressure and cook for 8 minutes, then reduce the pressure slowly. The potatoes should be on the brink of collapse. Take the tied herbs out of the soup and discard. Stir the cream into the soup off the heat, then using a hand blender blitz the soup until smooth or in batches in a food processor.

3 Reheat gently, if necessary, to serve, then ladle into bowls and scatter with parsley. Serve with crusty bread.

PER SERVING 279 kcals, protein 9g, carbs 20g, fat 18g, sat fat 11g, fibre 4g, sugar 2g, salt 0.6g

Chicken, sweetcorn & noodle soup

Comfort food without the calories – it's worth taking time to make a proper stock for this soup, which is quicker when using a pressure cooker.

TAKES 55 MINUTES • SERVES 8

1.3kg/3lb whole chicken
2 large carrots, chopped
2 large leeks, trimmed and finely sliced
2 corn on the cobs, corn kernels cut off
150g/5oz vermicelli noodles
small bunch parsley, finely chopped,
   to garnish

FOR THE STOCK

2 onions, quartered
1 leek, cut into chunks
2 carrots, thickly sliced
2 bay leaves
6 black peppercorns
few parsley stalks
4 celery sticks, roughly chopped
2 tbsp vegetable bouillon or
   1 vegetable stock cube

1 Put all the stock ingredients including the chicken in the pressure cooker, then cover everything with about 2 litres/3½ pints water. Close the lid, bring up to high pressure and cook for 25 minutes. Reduce the pressure slowly then remove the chicken to a plate to cool. Strain the stock through a sieve, skimming off as much fat as you can.
2 Rinse out the pressure cooker and put the stock back in. Add the carrots and leeks, then simmer for 10 minutes.
3 Meanwhile, shred the meat from the chicken, discarding the skin and bones. Add to the pan with the sweetcorn. Add the vermicelli noodles and simmer until the corn and noodles are cooked. Ladle into bowls and serve sprinkled with the parsley.

PER SERVING 288 kcals, protein 25g, carbs 28g, fat 9g, sat fat 3g, fibre 2g, sugar 5g, salt 0.71g

Split pea & green pea smoked-ham soup

A meal-in-a-bowl soup that's substantial enough to be served as a main course or hearty winter lunch.

TAKES 1 HOUR 10 MINUTES, PLUS OVERNIGHT SOAKING • SERVES 8

1kg/2lb 4oz gammon or ham hock
200g/7oz split peas, soaked overnight
2 onions, roughly chopped
2 carrots, roughly chopped
2 bay leaves
1 celery stick, roughly chopped
300g/10oz frozen peas
crusty bread and butter, to serve

1 Put the gammon or ham hock in the pressure cooker with 2 litres/3½ pints water and bring to the boil, uncovered. Remove from the heat and drain off the water – this helps to get rid of some of the saltiness. Re-cover with 2 litres/3½ pints cold water and put everything into the pan except the frozen peas. Close the lid and cook on high pressure for 50 minutes, then reduce the pressure slowly and remove the lid.

2 Lift out the ham, peel off and discard the skin. While it is still hot (wear a clean pair of rubber gloves), shred the meat. Remove the bay leaves from the soup and stir in the frozen peas. Simmer for 1 minute, then use a hand blender to blitz until smooth.

3 When you are ready to serve, mix the hot soup with most of the shredded ham. Serve in bowls with the remaining ham scattered on top, and eat with crusty bread and butter.

PER SERVING 292 kcals, protein 26g, carbs 23g, fat 11g, sat fat 4g, fibre 5g, sugar 5g, salt 3.56g

Carrot & coriander soup

Everyone will love this soup, which is simplicity itself to make and uses just a few low-cost ingredients.

TAKES 30 MINUTES • SERVES 4

1 tbsp vegetable oil
1 onion, chopped
1 tsp ground coriander
1 potato, chopped
450g/1lb carrots, peeled and chopped
1.2 litres/2 pints vegetable or chicken
    stock
handful coriander leaves (about ½ small
    supermarket pack)

1 Heat the oil in the pressure cooker, add the onion, then fry for 5 minutes until soft. Stir in the ground coriander and potato, then cook for 1 minute. Add the carrots and stock, close the lid, bring up to high pressure and cook for 5 minutes. Reduce the pressure slowly.
2 Remove the lid and add the coriander, reserving a few sprigs to garnish. Use a hand blender or food processor to blitz until smooth (you may need to do this in two batches in a processor). Return to the pan, if necessary add salt to taste, then reheat to serve, garnished with the reserved coriander.

PER SERVING 115 kcals, protein 3g, carbs 19g, fat 4g, sat fat 1g, fibre 5g, sugar 12g, salt 0.46g

Cauliflower-cheese soup

This comforting soup is perfect served in mugs at a chilly outdoor event like bonfire night.

TAKES 15 MINUTES ● **SERVES 6**

knob butter

1 large onion, finely chopped

1 potato, peeled and diced

1 large cauliflower (about 900g/2lb
  total), leaves trimmed and cut into
  florets

850ml/1½ pints vegetable stock (from
  a cube is fine)

400ml/14fl oz milk, plus extra to thin
  (optional)

100g/4oz mature Cheddar, diced

1 Heat the butter in the pressure cooker. Tip in the onion and cook until softened, about 5 minutes, stirring often. Add the potato and cook for 2 minutes more then add the cauliflower, stock, milk and some seasoning. Close the lid, bring up to high pressure and cook for 5 minutes, then reduce the pressure slowly.

2 Whizz in a food processor or crush with a potato masher until you get a thick, creamy soup. Top up with more milk to thin a little if serving in mugs. You can make ahead up to 2 days in advance, then cool, cover and leave in the fridge until needed, or freeze for up to 1 month. When ready to serve, warm through, ladle into mugs or bowls, top with the cheese pieces, then stir through before eating.

PER SERVING 188 kcals, protein 13g, carbs 13g, fat 10g, sat fat 5g, fibre 3g, sugar 9g, salt 0.82g

Velvety pumpkin soup

This soup has a beautiful texture because puréed pumpkin has to be one of the silkiest vegetables going.

TAKES 40 MINUTES ● SERVES 6

4 tbsp olive oil, plus extra for drizzling (optional)
2 onions, finely chopped
1kg/2lb 4oz pumpkin, peeled, deseeded and chopped into chunks
700ml/1¼ pint vegetable or chicken stock
142ml pot double cream
4 slices wholemeal seeded bread
handful pumpkin seeds, to garnish (optional)

1 Heat half the olive oil in the pressure cooker, then gently cook the onions for 5 minutes, until soft but not coloured. Add the pumpkin to the pan, then cook for a further 8–10 minutes, stirring occasionally until soft and golden.
2 Pour the stock into the pan, then season with some salt and black pepper. Close the lid, bring up to high pressure and cook for 5 minutes then reduce the pressure slowly. Remove the lid and pour the cream into the pan, bring back to the boil, then purée with a hand blender. The soup can be frozen for up to 2 months.
3 To make croutons, slice the crusts from the bread, then cut the bread into small cubes. Heat the remaining olive oil in a frying pan, then fry the bread until crisp. Add the seeds to the pan and cook for a few minutes until toasted. Reheat the soup if needed, taste for seasoning, then serve scattered with croutons and seeds and drizzled with olive oil, if you want.

PER SERVING 317 kcals, protein 6g, carbs 20g, fat 24g, sat fat 9g, fibre 4g, sugar 6g, salt 0.54g

Hearty mushroom soup

Dried mushrooms not only add a big flavour hit but their soaking liquid also doubles as a delicious mushroom stock.

TAKES 55 MINUTES ● SERVES 4–6

25g pack porcini mushrooms
2 tbsp olive oil
1 medium onion, finely diced
2 large carrots, diced
2 garlic cloves, finely chopped
1 tbsp chopped rosemary or 1 tsp dried
450g/1lb fresh mushrooms, such as chestnut, finely chopped
1.2 litres/2 pints vegetable stock (from a cube is fine), plus extra to thin (optional)
5 tbsp Marsala or dry sherry
2 tbsp tomato purée
100g/4oz pearl barley
grated Parmesan, to garnish (optional)

1 Put the porcini in a bowl with 250ml/9fl oz boiling water and leave to soak for 25 minutes.

2 Heat the oil in the pressure cooker and add the onion, carrots, garlic, rosemary and some seasoning. Fry for 5 minutes on a medium heat until softened. Drain and squeeze out the porcini, saving the liquid, and finely chop. Tip the porcini into the pan with the fresh mushrooms. Fry for another 5 minutes, then add the stock, Marsala or sherry, tomato purée, barley and strained porcini liquid.

3 Close the lid, bring it up to high pressure and cook for 20 minutes, then fast-release the pressure. The barley should be soft; if not, simmer for a few minutes more, adding more liquid if it is too thick. Serve in bowls with Parmesan sprinkled over, if desired.

PER SERVING (6) 245 kcals, protein 8g, carbs 35g, fat 7g, sat fat 1g, fibre 3g, sugar 10g, salt 1.13g

Roasted red-pepper shots

This recipe makes 30 canapé-sized shots for summer entertaining or about eight as a starter for a sit-down lunch.

TAKES 20 MINUTES • MAKES 30 SHOTS OR SERVES 8

1 tbsp olive oil
1 onion, roughly chopped
3 garlic cloves, crushed
1 tbsp sugar
2 tbsp red pepper pesto
400g can peeled plum tomatoes
480g jar roasted red peppers
450ml/16fl oz vegetable stock
basil leaves, to garnish (optional)

1 Heat the oil in the pressure cooker. Put the chopped onion in and cook for 8–10 minutes, then add the crushed garlic cloves, the sugar and red pepper pesto, and cook for 1–2 minutes. Tip in the plum tomatoes, then drain and chop the roasted red peppers and add these too. Pour in the vegetable stock, close the lid, bring up to high pressure and cook for 5 minutes, then reduce the pressure slowly.

2 Season, then blend until smooth with a hand blender. To serve, reheat gently in a pan, or microwave on high for a few minutes, stirring often, until hot. Serve in shot glasses, garnished with basil leaves, if you like.

PER SHOT 15 kcals, protein 1g, carbs 2g, fat 1g, sat fat none, fibre none, sugar 1g, salt 0.12g

Italian vegetable soup

Mix and match your vegetable selection to suit what's in season. Garden peas, broad beans or shredded cabbage would all work well.

TAKES 45 MINUTES • SERVES 8

1 tbsp olive oil

2 each onions and carrots, chopped

4 celery sticks, chopped

2 tbsp caster sugar

4 garlic cloves, crushed

2 tbsp tomato purée

2 bay leaves

few sprigs thyme

3 courgettes, chopped

400g can butter beans, drained and rinsed

400g can chopped tomatoes

1.2 litres/2 pints vegetable stock

100g/4oz Parmesan or vegetarian equivalent, grated

140g/5oz small pasta shapes

small bunch basil, shredded, to garnish

1 Heat the oil in a pressure cooker and gently cook the onions, carrots and celery for 20 minutes, until soft. Add the sugar, garlic, tomato purée, herbs and courgettes, and cook on a medium heat for 4–5 minutes until they just brown a little.

2 Pour in the beans, tomatoes and stock, close the lid, bring up to high pressure and cook for 10 minutes, then fast-release the pressure. If you're freezing the soup, cool and do so now. The soup will freeze for up to 1 month. If not, add half the Parmesan or vegetarian equivalent and the pasta, and simmer for 6–8 minutes, uncovered, until the pasta is cooked. Sprinkle with basil and the remaining Parmesan to serve. If frozen, defrost and reheat before adding the pasta and cheese and continuing as above.

PER SERVING 215 kcals, protein 11g, carbs 30g, fat 6g, sat fat 3g, fibre 5g, sugar 12g, salt 1.06g

Leek, bacon & potato soup

This soup will keep in the fridge for a couple of days. You can also freeze it for up to 1 month, just be sure not to add the cream until you reheat it.

TAKES 30 MINUTES ● SERVES 4–6

25g/1oz butter

7 rashers streaky bacon, 3 chopped, 4 left whole

1 onion, chopped

400g pack trimmed leeks, sliced and well washed

3 medium potatoes, peeled and diced

1.4 litres/2½ pints hot vegetable stock

142ml pot single cream

toasted or warm crusty bread, to serve

1 Melt the butter in the pressure cooker and fry the chopped bacon and onion, stirring, until they start to turn golden. Tip in the leeks and potatoes, stir well, then cover and turn down the heat. Cook gently for 5 minutes, shaking the pan every now and then to make sure that the mixture doesn't catch.

2 Pour in the stock, season well, close the lid, bring up to low pressure and cook for 12 minutes. Reduce the pressure slowly then blend with a hand blender or in a food processor in batches until smooth. Return to the pan, pour in the cream and stir well.

3 While the soup is cooking, grill the remaining 4 bacon rashers until crisp and drain on kitchen paper. Taste and season if necessary.

4 Serve the soup scattered with the crisp bacon and eat with toasted or warm crusty bread on the side.

PER SERVING (6) 175 kcals, protein 6g, carbs 15g, fat 11g, sat fat 6g, fibre 4g, sugar 5g, salt 0.68g

Indian winter soup

A warming soup to suit everyone – it's vegetarian, high in fibre and low in fat.

TAKES 30 MINUTES • SERVES 4–6

2 tbsp vegetable oil
½ tsp brown mustard seeds
1 tsp cumin seeds
2 green chillies, deseeded and finely
    chopped
1 bay leaf
2 whole cloves
1 small cinnamon stick
½ tsp turmeric powder
1 large onion, chopped
2 garlic cloves, finely chopped
1 parsnip, cut into chunks
200g/7oz butternut squash, cut into
    chunks
200g/7oz sweet potato, cut into chunks
1 tsp paprika
1 tsp ground coriander
225g/8oz red split lentils
100g/4oz pearl barley
2 tomatoes, chopped
small bunch coriander, chopped
1 tsp grated ginger
1 tsp lemon juice

1 Heat the oil in a pressure cooker. Fry the mustard seeds, cumin seeds, chillies, bay leaf, cloves, cinnamon and turmeric until fragrant and the seeds start to crackle. Tip in the onion and garlic, then cook for 5 minutes until soft. Stir in the remaining vegetables and mix thoroughly, making sure the vegetables are fully coated with the oil and spices. Sprinkle in the paprika, ground coriander and seasoning, and stir again.

2 Add the lentils, pearl barley, tomatoes and 1.7 litres/3 pints water. Close the lid, bring up to high pressure and cook for 20 minutes, then reduce the pressure slowly and stir in the chopped coriander, ginger and lemon juice, and serve.

PER SERVING (6) 445 kcals, protein 19g, carbs 80g, fat 8g, sat fat 1g, fibre 8g, sugar 13g, salt 0.14g

Tomato soup with gremolata

A great soup to make if you find yourself with a glut of ripe tomatoes.

TAKES 40 MINUTES • SERVES 4

4 tbsp olive oil
1 onion, chopped
2 garlic cloves, crushed
1.4kg/3lb 3oz tomatoes
2 tbsp sugar
2 tbsp white wine vinegar

FOR THE GREMOLATA

zest and juice 1 lemon
3 tbsp olive oil
2 garlic cloves, crushed
bunch flat-leaf parsley, finely chopped

1 Heat the olive oil in a pressure cooker and fry the onion and garlic on a low heat for 8 minutes. Roughly chop the tomatoes and add along with the sugar, vinegar, 400ml/14fl oz water and some seasoning. Close the lid, bring up to high pressure and cook for 15 minutes, then reduce the pressure slowly.

2 Whizz with a hand-held blender until smooth. For an ultra-smooth, dinner party-style soup, you can pass the liquid through a fine sieve, but this is quite fiddly and your blender will give perfectly good results. Add a drop more water if it is too thick.

3 For the gremolata, mix together the lemon zest, juice, olive oil, garlic and parsley, then serve on top of the soup.

PER SERVING 307 kcals, protein 4g, carbs 27g, fat 21g, sat fat 3g, fibre 6g, sugar 25g, salt 0.13g

Spiced root-vegetable soup

This vegetarian soup will keep well in the fridge and can be easily transported and reheated at work for a filling lunch.

TAKES 30 MINUTES • SERVES 4

2 tbsp olive oil
2 onions, finely chopped
2 sweet potatoes, chopped
2 carrots, chopped
2 parsnips, chopped
1 red chilli, roughly chopped
1 tbsp ground cumin
75g/2½oz dried green lentils
1 litre/1¾ pints vegetable stock, plus
  extra to thin (optional)
425ml/¾ pint milk
100g/4oz Greek yogurt
1 tbsp coriander leaves, chopped

1 Heat the olive oil in the pressure cooker. Add the onions and fry for 5 minutes until soft. Tip in the remaining vegetables and cook for another 5 minutes, adding the chilli and cumin for the final 2 minutes.

2 Add the lentils and stock to the pan and close the lid. Bring up to high pressure and cook for 15 minutes, then reduce the pressure slowly. Add the milk and blitz until smooth with a hand blender or in a food processor in batches, adding a little extra water or stock, if necessary. The soup can now be chilled and stored in the fridge for 3 days or frozen for 6 months.

3 Reheat until piping hot. Ladle into bowls and serve with a dollop of Greek yogurt and a sprinkle of chopped coriander.

PER SERVING 387 kcals, protein 15g, carbs 56g, fat 14g, sat fat 3g, fibre 9g, sugar 22g, salt 2.81g

Butternut & harissa houmous

A delicious dip to serve as a casual starter or to take to work for lunch spread on toast or for dipping in with vegetable sticks.

TAKES 20 MINUTES ● SERVES 6

½ butternut squash (about 400g/14oz total), peeled and cut into 2.5cm/1in pieces
3 garlic cloves, unpeeled
2 tbsp olive oil
3 tbsp tahini paste
1 tbsp harissa, plus a little extra for drizzling
400g can chickpeas, drained and rinsed
flatbread, to serve

1 Put the butternut squash and garlic cloves in a pressure cooker, season well and add 100ml/3½fl oz water. Close the lid, bring up to high pressure and cook for 6 minutes then release the pressure slowly.

2 Tip the squash into a food processor with any juices from the pan. Add the garlic cloves, squeezed out of their skins. Add the remaining ingredients, season with some salt and blend to a paste. Scrape the houmous into a bowl. Drizzle with extra harissa and serve with flatbread alongside.

PER SERVING 155 kcals, protein 4g, carbs 13g, fat 9g, sat fat 1g, fibre 3g, sugar 3g, salt 0.4g

Lime & coconut dhal

Here's a great side dish to serve as part of a bigger vegetarian Indian feast.

TAKES 15 MINUTES • SERVES 8

1–2 tbsp mild curry paste
160ml can coconut cream
zest 1 lime, plus a squeeze of juice
1 heaped tsp brown sugar
400g can brown lentils, drained
handful chopped coriander leaves, plus
    extra to garnish (optional)
2 warmed naan bread, cut into fingers

1 Heat the curry paste in the pressure cooker for 1 minute. Pour in the coconut cream and stir to combine. Add the lime zest, brown sugar and lentils. Close the lid, bring up to high pressure and cook for 5 minutes then reduce the pressure slowly.
2 Remove the lid and add the squeeze of lime juice and some seasoning, stir through some chopped coriander and serve with warmed naan breads. Sprinkle extra coriander on the dhal, if you like. Great warm or at room temperature.

PER SERVING 104 kcals, protein 3g, carbs 7g, fat 8g, sat fat 6g, fibre 2g, sugar 2g, salt 0.39g

Warm Mexican-bean dip with tortilla chips

This dip could be served as an element of a larger Mexican meal and has the added bonus of being superhealthy. Make it ahead and reheat just before guests arrive.

TAKES 20 MINUTES • SERVES 8

1 onion, chopped
1 tbsp olive oil
1 tsp soft brown sugar
1 tsp red wine vinegar
1 tsp Cajun seasoning
400g can mixed beans, drained and
   rinsed
400g can chopped tomatoes with garlic
handful grated Cheddar
100g/4oz tortilla chips
chopped avocado, to garnish (optional)

1 Fry the onion in the olive oil in a pressure cooker until soft. Add the sugar, wine vinegar and Cajun seasoning. Cook for 1 minute then add the mixed beans, the chopped tomatoes and 50ml/2fl oz water. Close the lid, bring up to high pressure and cook for 10 minutes then reduce the pressure slowly.

2 Scatter the grated Cheddar on to the tortilla chips. Microwave on High or grill for 1 minute until the cheese has melted. Serve alongside the dip (top with some chopped avocado, if you like).

PER SERVING 144 kcals, protein 6g, carbs 16g, fat 7g, sat fat 2g, fibre 3g, sugar 3g, salt 0.76g

Red cabbage with beetroot

This cabbage dish goes particularly well with roast duck, goose, game or pork and also complements cold cuts like ham.

TAKES 45 MINUTES • SERVES 8

85g/3oz golden caster sugar

750g/1lb 10oz red cabbage, quartered, cored and thinly sliced

2 large onions, halved and thinly sliced

2 eating apples, such as Cox's, peeled, quartered, cored and very thickly sliced

4 raw beetroot, peeled and cut into thin wedges

2 cinnamon sticks, snapped in half

3 star anise

300ml/½ pint red wine

100ml/3½fl oz vinegar

1 vegetable stock cube, crumbled

25g/1oz butter

1 Mix the sugar with 1 teaspoon salt and plenty of black pepper. In a pressure cooker layer up a handful of the cabbage, onions, apples and beetroot with the spices, and sprinkle with some of the seasoned sugar, repeating with the layers until all the ingredients are used up.

2 Mix the wine, vinegar and stock cube, pour over the cabbage and dot the butter on top. Close the lid, bring up to high pressure, cook for 20 minutes, then fast-release the pressure. Stir well; the mixture will have reduced and softened the cabbage.

PER SERVING 138 kcals, protein 3g, carbs 23g, fat 3g, sat fat 2g, fibre 5g, sugar 21g, salt 1.1g

Braised cabbage & carrots

Give cabbage a smarter look by cutting it into wedges – it's actually easier to serve and takes less time to prepare.

TAKES 10 MINUTES • SERVES 4

small knob butter
2 carrots, cut into batons
1 Savoy cabbage, cut into 8 wedges
    attached at the core
150ml/¼ pint vegetable stock

1 Heat the butter in the pressure cooker, then add the carrots and sizzle for 1 minute until glossy and coated.
2 Nestle the cabbage wedges snugly in the pan and pour over the stock. Cover with the lid and cook on high pressure for 5 minutes, then fast-release the pressure and remove the lid. You should have soft, wilted cabbage and tender carrots.

PER SERVING 58 kcals, protein 3g, carbs 7g, fat 2g, sat fat 1g, fibre 5g, sugar 7g, salt 0.2g

Moroccan tomato & chickpea stew with couscous

This soupy stew is really filling as well as healthy. It's ideal for vegans and mostly made from storecupboard ingredients.

TAKES 45 MINUTES ● SERVES 4

75g/2½oz couscous
3 tbsp olive oil
700ml/1¼ pints hot vegetable stock
1 large onion, finely chopped
1 carrot, chopped into small cubes
4 garlic cloves, crushed
½ finger sized piece ginger, peeled and
   finely chopped
1–2 tbsp ras-el-hanout spice mix
1 tbsp harissa paste, plus extra to taste
   (optional)
400g can chopped tomatoes
400g can chickpeas, drained and rinsed
juice ½ lemon
roughly chopped coriander, to garnish

1 Tip the couscous into a bowl, season with some salt and pepper and stir through 1 tablespoon of the oil. Pour over enough hot stock just to cover, then cover the bowl with cling film and set aside.

2 Heat the rest of the oil in the pressure cooker and cook the onion and carrot gently for 8 minutes until soft. Add in the garlic and ginger, and cook for 2 minutes more, then stir in the harissa and ras-el-hanout, and cook for another minute. Pour in the tomatoes and remaining stock, and give everything a good stir. Season, add the chickpeas, close the lid, bring up to low pressure and cook for 20 minutes. Release the pressure slowly, remove the lid then pour over the lemon juice.

3 Uncover the couscous and fluff up with a fork. Spoon the stew into bowls, top each with a mound of couscous, scatter with coriander and serve with extra harissa for those who want it.

PER SERVING 265 kcals, protein 7g, carbs 33g, fat 10g, sat fat 1g, fibre 6g, sugar 10g, salt 1.2g

Chilli & tangerine braised lentils

Being able quickly to cook dried pulses, like lentils, which normally require a bit of time, is one of the best things about owning a pressure cooker.

TAKES 35 MINUTES • **SERVES 8**

4 tbsp olive oil
1 carrot, finely chopped
1 onion, finely chopped
1 celery stick, finely chopped
2 red chillies, deseeded and finely
    chopped
2 garlic cloves, finely chopped
450g/1lb Puy lentils, rinsed
1.2 litres/2 pints vegetable stock
zest and juice 3 tangerines
2 tbsp crème fraîche
1 bunch flat-leaf parsley, chopped

1 Heat the olive oil in the pressure cooker. Add the carrot, onion, celery, chillies and garlic, and cook for 5–10 minutes until the veg begin to soften. Add the rinsed lentils. Pour on the stock and most of the tangerine juice, close the lid, bring up to high pressure and cook for 15 minutes. Fast-release the pressure and taste the lentils; if they need a little longer, simmer for a few minutes more, uncovered.
2 Remove from the heat and stir in the tangerine zest and remaining juice. Season with some salt and pepper, and allow to cool a little before stirring through the crème fraîche and parsley. Serve warm or at room temperature.

PER SERVING 259 kcals, protein 15g, carbs 31g, fat 9g, sat fat 2g, fibre 6g, sugar 5g, salt 1.4g

Gigantes plaki

These Greek beans make a great mezze dish served with crusty bread, or serve them with grilled or roast lamb.

TAKES 1 HOUR, PLUS OVERNIGHT SOAKING • SERVES 4

400g/14oz dried butter beans
3 tbsp olive oil, plus extra to drizzle
1 Spanish onion, finely chopped
2 garlic cloves, finely chopped
2 tbsp tomato purée
800g/1lb 12oz ripe tomatoes, skins removed and roughly chopped
50ml/2fl oz vegetable stock
1 tsp sugar
1 tsp dried oregano
pinch ground cinnamon
2 tbsp chopped flat-leaf parsley leaves, plus extra to garnish

1 Soak the beans overnight in plenty of water. Drain, rinse, then put the beans in the pressure cooker covered with water. Close the lid, bring up to high pressure and cook for 12 minutes. Fast-reduce the pressure, then drain the beans and set aside. Clean the pressure cooker.

2 Heat the olive oil in the pressure cooker and tip in the onion and garlic. Cook over a medium heat for 10 minutes until softened but not browned. Add the tomato purée, cook for a further minute, add the remaining ingredients, then simmer for 2–3 minutes. Season, then stir in the beans. Close the lid and bring up to high pressure, cook for 3 minutes then reduce the pressure slowly. Tip the beans into an ovenproof serving dish and eat straight away, with a scatter of parsley and a drizzle of oil, or leave to go cold.

3 To reheat, heat oven to 180C/160C fan/gas 4 then bake the beans for 20 minutes, uncovered, until hot. Serve as above.

PER SERVING 431 kcals, protein 22g, carbs 66g, fat 11g, sat fat 1g, fibre 19g, sugar 15g, salt 0.2g

Lentil ragout

A superhealthy vegetarian version of Bolognese sauce that can be served with pasta or used as a base for a veggie shepherd's pie.

TAKES 50 MINUTES ● SERVES 6

3 tbsp olive oil
2 onions, finely chopped
3 carrots, finely chopped
3 celery sticks, finely chopped
3 garlic cloves, crushed
500g bag red split lentils
2 x 400g cans chopped tomatoes
2 tbsp tomato purée
2 tsp each dried oregano and thyme
3 bay leaves
1 litre/1¾ pints vegetable stock
500g/1lb 2oz spaghetti
Parmesan or vegetarian cheese,
    grated, to garnish

1 Heat the oil in the pressure cooker and add the onions, carrots, celery and garlic. Cook gently for 15–20 minutes until everything is softened. Stir in the lentils, chopped tomatoes, tomato purée, herbs and stock. Close the lid, bring up to high pressure and cook for 15 minutes. Reduce the pressure slowly – the lentils should be tender and saucy, but splash in a little water if you need to loosen it. Season to taste.

2 If eating straight away, keep on a low heat while you cook the spaghetti, according to the pack instructions. Alternatively, cool the sauce and chill for up to 3 days or freeze for up to 3 months. Simply defrost portions overnight at room temperature, then reheat gently to serve.

3 Drain the pasta well, divide among bowls or plates, spoon the sauce over the top and grate over some cheese.

PER SERVING 662 kcals, protein 33g, carbs 120g, fat 9g, sat fat 1g, fibre 10g, sugar 14g, salt 1.05g

Potato curry with lime & cucumber raita

If you're missing meat, this curry is also delicious served with some spiced-lamb chops or slow-roasted spiced-lamb leg.

TAKES 45 MINUTES • SERVES 5

2 tbsp sunflower or vegetable oil
1 tbsp brown or black mustard seeds
3 long dried red Indian chillies
12–15 freeze dried curry leaves
2 onions, sliced
2 tsp each ground coriander, garam masala and turmeric powder
500g/1lb 2oz tomatoes, quartered
800g/1lb 12oz potatoes, peeled and cut into very large chunks
400ml can coconut milk
naan bread, rotis or chapatis, to serve

FOR THE RAITA

150g pot natural yogurt
zest and juice 1 lime
½ cucumber, deseeded and coarsely grated
small handful coriander leaves, roughly chopped

1 Heat the oil in the pressure cooker and fry the mustard seeds, chillies and curry leaves until the seeds start to pop. Add the onions and fry until softened and starting to brown. Stir in the spices, add the tomatoes and fry for 5 minutes. Add the potatoes and stir to coat. Pour in the coconut milk with 100ml/3fl oz water, close the lid, bring up to high pressure and cook for 5 minutes, then fast-release the pressure – the potatoes should be just tender.

2 To make the raita, mix all the ingredients together with some seasoning.

3 If the curry looks a little too saucy, scoop out the potatoes with a slotted spoon into another dish, then boil the sauce until reduced a little. Stir the potatoes back in to heat through, and season well (this curry needs a good sprinkling of salt). Serve with warmed Indian bread and a dollop of raita.

PER SERVING 383 kcals, protein 9g, carbs 43g, fat 21g, sat fat 13g, fibre 4g, sugar 12g, salt 0.35g

Vegetable & bean chilli

This healthy veggie chilli makes for a quick and satisfying supper, crammed with pulses and colourful fresh vegetables.

TAKES 30 MINUTES • SERVES 4

1 tbsp olive oil
1 garlic clove, finely chopped
thumb-sized piece ginger, finely
    chopped
1 large onion, chopped
2 courgettes, diced
1 red pepper, deseeded and chopped
1 yellow pepper, deseeded and
    chopped
1 tbsp chilli powder
100g/4oz red split lentils, washed and
    drained
1 tbsp tomato purée
2 x 400g cans chopped tomatoes
195g can sweetcorn, drained
420g can butter beans, drained and
    rinsed
400g can kidney beans in water,
    drained and rinsed

1 Heat the oil in the pressure cooker. Cook the garlic, ginger, onion, courgettes and peppers for about 5 minutes until starting to soften. Add the chilli powder and cook for 1 minute more.

2 Stir in the lentils, tomato purée, tomatoes and 250ml/7fl oz water. Close the lid, bring up to high pressure and cook for 15 minutes. Fast-release the pressure then remove the lid and stir in the sweetcorn and beans, and simmer, uncovered, until everything is piping hot.

PER SERVING 361 kcals, protein 21g, carbs 61g, fat 6g, sat fat 1g, fibre 13g, sugar 21g, salt 1.34g

Tomato & hidden-veg sauce

This smooth sauce is a good way to get kids to eat more vegetables, and you can always add a touch of spice for adults.

TAKES 1 HOUR 10 MINUTES
- **SERVES 4**

1 tsp olive oil
1 large onion, chopped
2 celery sticks, chopped
2 carrots, chopped
1 leek, chopped
2 peppers, deseeded and chopped
2 x 400g cans chopped tomatoes with garlic
1 tbsp each caster sugar and balsamic vinegar
300g/10oz pasta shapes
Parmesan, shaved, and rocket leaves, to garnish (optional)

1 Heat the oil in a pressure cooker and gently cook the onion, celery, carrots and leek until soft, about 20 minutes. Add in the peppers and cook for 10 minutes more, then tip in the sugar, tomatoes and vinegar. Close the lid, bring up to high pressure and cook for 10 minutes, then slow-release the pressure.

2 Cook the pasta according to the pack instructions. Meanwhile, blitz the sauce with a hand blender until smooth, season and return to the heat to keep warm while the pasta cooks. Drain the pasta and toss through the sauce. Serve in bowls topped with shaved Parmesan and rocket leaves, if you like.

PER SERVING 381 kcals, protein 14g, carbs 79g, fat 3g, sat fat 1g, fibre 8g, sugar 22g, salt 0.35g

Caponata

This Sicilian aubergine dish is typically served as starter with bruschetta, but it also makes a wonderful side dish.

TAKES 1 HOUR • SERVES 6–8

100ml/3½fl oz olive oil

3 large aubergines, cut into 2.5cm/1in cubes

2 long shallots, chopped

4 large plum tomatoes, chopped

2 tsp capers, soaked if salted

50g/2oz raisins

4 celery sticks, sliced

50ml/2fl oz red wine vinegar

handful toasted pine nuts and basil leaves, to garnish

FOR THE BRUSCHETTA

8 slices ciabatta

olive oil, for drizzling

1 garlic clove

1 Pour most of the olive oil into a pressure cooker, put over a medium heat and add the aubergines. Cook for 15–20 minutes until soft, stirring often.

2 Scoop the aubergines out of the pan. Heat the rest of the oil in the pan, add the shallots and cook for about 5 minutes until they are soft and translucent. Add the tomatoes and cook slowly, until a soft mush, then return the aubergines to the pan. Put in the capers, raisins, celery and vinegar, season well, and cover with a lid. Close the lid, bring up to high pressure and cook for 10 minutes, then fast-release the pressure. Stir gently; the vegetables should be very tender. Once cooked, leave to cool slighlty.

3 To make the bruschetta, heat a griddle pan and drizzle the bread with olive oil. Griddle until toasted, rub with a garlic clove and season. Serve the caponata scattered with the basil leaves and pine nuts, with bruschetta on the side.

PER SERVING (8) 235 kcals, protein 4g, carbs 20g, fat 15g, sat fat 2g, fibre 5g, sugar 8g, salt 0.4g

Somerset stew

Serve this bean stew with some cheesy mash for a comforting but meat-free meal.

TAKES 35 MINUTES ● SERVES 4

1 tbsp vegetable oil
1 onion, finely chopped
1 garlic clove, finely chopped
1 large carrot, finely chopped
1 leek, chopped
1 tbsp tomato purée
400g can chopped tomatoes
200g can butter beans, drained and
    rinsed
400g can flageolet beans, drained and
    rinsed
200ml/7fl oz dry cider
250ml/9fl oz vegetable stock
few sprigs thyme, leaves only
cheesy mash, to serve

1 Heat the oil in a pressure cooker and fry the onion, garlic, carrot and leek until soft but not coloured. Add the tomato purée, chopped tomatoes, butter beans, flageolet beans, cider, stock and thyme. Close the lid, bring up to high pressure and cook for 10 minutes. Release the pressure slowly.

2 The stew should be thickened and the veg tender; if the sauce isn't thick enough, simmer gently over a low heat, uncovered. Serve with cheesy mash.

PER SERVING 169 kcals, protein 9g, carbs 24g, fat 4g, sat fat none, fibre 7g, sugar 10g, salt 0.99g

Black bean chilli

This chilli is great for casual entertaining – just lay everything out and let people add their own toppings.

TAKES 40 MINUTES ● **SERVES 6**

2 tbsp olive oil
4 garlic cloves, finely chopped
2 large onions, chopped
3 tbsp sweet pimentón (Spanish paprika) or mild chilli powder
3 tbsp ground cumin
3 tbsp cider vinegar
2 tbsp brown sugar
2 x 400g cans chopped tomatoes
2 x 400g cans black beans, drained and rinsed

TO SERVE
cooked rice
a few, or one, of the following:
  crumbled feta, chopped spring onions, sliced radishes, avocado chunks, soured cream

1 Heat the olive oil in the pressure cooker, and fry the garlic and onions for 5 minutes until almost softened. Add the pimentón or chilli powder and the cumin, cook for a few minutes, then add the vinegar, sugar, tomatoes and some seasoning. Close the lid, bring up to high pressure and cook for 10 minutes, then slow-release the pressure.

2 Pour in the beans and simmer for another 10 minutes until the sauce is thicker. Serve with rice and the accompaniments of your choice in small bowls for people to help themselves.

PER SERVING 339 kcals, protein 17g, carbs 50g, fat 10g, sat fat 1g, fibre 8g, sugar 20g, salt 1.45g

Yellow lentil & coconut curry with cauliflower

Use a curry paste that suits your taste and chilli resistance as this dish works just as well with Indian flavourings as it does with Thai.

TAKES 45 MINUTES ● **SERVES 4**

1 tbsp vegetable oil

1 onion, thinly sliced

2 garlic cloves, crushed

thumb-sized piece ginger, finely
    chopped

3 tbsp your favourite curry paste

200g/7oz yellow lentils, rinsed

1.5 litres/2¾ pints vegetable stock

3 tbsp unsweetened desiccated
    coconut, plus extra to sprinkle
    (optional)

1 medium cauliflower, broken into little
    florets

cooked basmati rice and sprinkling
    coriander leaves, plus mango
    chutney and naan bread (optional),
    to serve

1 Heat the oil in the pressure cooker, then add the onion, garlic and ginger. Cook for 5 minutes, add the curry paste, then stir-fry for 1 minute before adding the lentils, stock and coconut. Close the lid, bring up to high pressure and cook for 15 minutes.

2 Fast-release the pressure and stir in the cauliflower, and simmer uncovered for 10 minutes until the cauliflower is tender.

3 Spoon the rice into four bowls, top with the curry and sprinkle with coriander leaves and the extra coconut, and serve with mango chutney and naan bread alongside, if you like.

PER SERVING 356 kcals, protein 18g, carbs 33g, fat 17g, sat fat 9g, fibre 10g, sugar 9g, salt 1.4g

Creamy barley & squash risotto

Follow the same quantities of barley to stock and you can add whatever you want instead of the squash – mushrooms, asparagus or broad beans.

TAKES 45 MINUTES • SERVES 6

1 tbsp butter
1 onion, finely chopped
1 small butternut squash (600–700g/
    1lb 5oz–1lb 9oz), peeled and diced
    into small chunks
2 garlic cloves, crushed
150ml white wine
400g/14oz pearl barley
1.2 litres/2 pints hot vegetable stock
1 tbsp mascarpone
50g/2oz Parmesan, grated
large handful parsley leaves, chopped
snipped chives, to serve

1 Heat the butter in a pressure cooker. Add the onion and cook very gently, stirring occasionally, until the onion is soft, about 10 minutes. Stir in the squash and the garlic, and cook for 1 minute more. Splash in the white wine and boil down. Add the barley, give it a stir and pour in the stock. Close the lid, bring up to high pressure and cook for 20 minutes.

2 Release the pressure slowly and stir through the mascarpone, half the Parmesan and all the parsley, then season. Spoon into bowls and scatter with the remaining Parmesan and the chives.

PER SERVING 383 kcals, protein 11g, carbs 65g, fat 7g, sat fat 4g, fibre 4g, sugar 8g, salt 1g

Ratatouille

Make the most of summer vegetables with this classic French vegetarian dish that goes with just about anything.

TAKES 45 MINUTES ● SERVES 4

4 large ripe tomatoes
5 tbsp olive oil
2 large aubergines, cut into large chunks
4 small courgettes, cut into large chunks
2 red or yellow peppers, deseeded and cut into chunks
small bunch basil
1 medium onion, peeled and thinly sliced
3 garlic cloves, peeled and crushed
1 tbsp red wine vinegar
1 tsp caster sugar

1 Score a small cross on the base of each tomato, then put them into a bowl. Cover with boiling water, leave for 20 seconds, then drain and cover with cold water. Leave to cool, then peel away the skin. Quarter the tomatoes, scrape away and discard the seeds with a spoon, then roughly chop the flesh. Set aside.

2 Heat 2 tablespoons of the olive oil in a pressure cooker and brown the aubergines until soft then set them aside. Fry the courgettes in a tablespoon of the oil until golden. Repeat with the peppers.

3 Tear up the basil leaves and set aside. Cook the onion in the pan for 5 minutes. Add the garlic and fry for a further minute. Stir in the vinegar and sugar, then tip in the tomatoes and half the basil. Return the vegetables to the pan with 50ml/2fl oz water, close the lid, bring up to high pressure and cook for 3 minutes, then fast-release the pressure. Leave to cool slightly then serve with the basil.

PER SERVING 241 kcals, protein 6g, carbs 20g, fat 16g, sat fat 2g, fibre 8g, sugar 18g, salt 0.05g

One-pan prawn & tomato curry

You can also make this curry using diced boneless skinless chicken breasts instead of the prawns – it just takes a little longer to cook.

TAKES 45 MINUTES • SERVES 4

2 tbsp sunflower oil
1 large onion, chopped
large piece ginger, crushed
4 garlic cloves, crushed
½ red chilli, finely chopped
1 tsp golden caster sugar
1 tsp black mustard seeds
1 tsp ground cumin
1 tsp ground coriander
1 tsp turmeric powder
1 tbsp garam masala
2 tsp malt vinegar
400g can chopped tomatoes
400g/14oz peeled raw king prawns
small bunch coriander, chopped
basmati rice, natural yogurt and mango
   chutney, to serve

1 Heat the oil in the pressure cooker and cook the onion for 8–10 minutes until it starts to turn golden. Add the ginger, garlic and chilli, and cook for 1–2 minutes. Stir in the sugar and spices for 1 minute, then splash in the vinegar and tomatoes. Season with some salt, close the lid, bring up to high pressure and cook for 4 minutes. Reduce the pressure slowly.

2 Stir in the prawns and simmer for 8-10 minutes, uncovered, on a low heat until the prawns are cooked through – if the sauce gets really thick, add a splash of water. Remove from the heat, stir though most of the coriander. Serve scattered with the remaining coriander and the rice, yogurt and chutney in separate bowls.

PER SERVING 217 kcals, protein 22g, carbs 16g, fat 8g, sat fat 1g, fibre 3g, sugar 9g, salt 0.66g

Thai-style steamed fish

Fish can be tricky in a pressure cooker but steaming it in a foil package is a good way to do it. Use these timings for any fish fillets you want.

TAKES 25 MINUTES • SERVES 2

2 trout fillets (about 140g/5oz each)
small knob ginger, peeled and chopped
1 small garlic clove, chopped
1 small red chilli (not bird's eye),
    deseeded and finely chopped
grated zest and juice 1 lime
3 baby pak choi, each quartered
    lengthways
2 tbsp soy sauce
rice or noodles, to serve

1 Nestle the fish fillets side by side on a large square of foil and scatter the ginger, garlic, chilli and lime zest over them. Drizzle the lime juice on top and then scatter the pieces of pak choi around on top of the fish. Pour the soy sauce over the pak choi then fold over and loosely seal the foil to make a package.

2 Pour 100ml/3½fl oz water in the pressure cooker and then put a trivet in the pan. Put the foil package on top of the trivet. Close the lid, bring up to high pressure and cook for 4 minutes then reduce the pressure slowly. Carefully remove the package from the pressure cooker on to a platter and open at the table, served with rice or noodles.

PER SERVING 199kcals, protein 29g, carbs 4g, fat 7g, sat fat 2g, fibre none, sugar none, salt 3.25g

Salmon Provençal

Use the pressure cooker to make a quick pepper stew, then poach the fish gently in the stew so it doesn't overcook.

TAKES 35 MINUTES • SERVES 4

1 tbsp olive oil
3 mixed peppers, deseeded and sliced
1 large onion, thinly sliced
400g/14oz baby potatoes, unpeeled
    and halved
2 tsp smoked paprika
2 garlic cloves, sliced
2 tsp dried thyme
400g can chopped tomatoes
4 salmon fillets
1 tbsp chopped parsley, to garnish
    (optional)

1 Heat the oil in the pressure cooker and add the peppers, onion and potatoes. Cook, stirring regularly, for 5–8 minutes until golden. Then add the paprika, garlic, thyme and tomatoes. Close the lid, bring up to high pressure and cook for 5 minutes then fast-release the pressure.

2 Season the stew and lay the salmon on top, skin-side down. Put the lid back on, to cover but not for pressure, and simmer gently for another 8 minutes until the salmon is cooked through. Scatter with parsley, if you like, and serve.

PER SERVING 414 kcals, protein 33g, carbs 29g, fat 19g, sat fat 4g, fibre 5g, sugar 11g, salt 0.33g

Simmered squid

This is delicious as a main course served with rice or as tapas at a drinks party with cocktail sticks and some bread to mop up the juices.

TAKES 55 MINUTES ● SERVES 4 AS A MAIN, 6 AS A STARTER

1 tbsp olive oil, plus extra for drizzling
1kg/2lb 4oz squid, cleaned and cut into thick rings, tentacles left whole
2 onions, chopped
3 garlic cloves, sliced
pinch chilli flakes
1 tsp fennel seeds
3 bay leaves
1 tbsp rosemary leaves, roughly chopped
pinch sugar
3 tbsp red wine vinegar
400g can chopped tomatoes
large glass red wine (about 200ml/7fl oz)

TO GARNISH

handful chopped coriander leaves
zest ½ orange, finely grated

1 Heat the olive oil in the pressure cooker and add the squid, onions and garlic. Add the dry ingredients and simmer until all the juices have evaporated and the onions are tender, about 10 minutes. Add the vinegar and chopped tomatoes, simmer for 1 minute, then pour over the red wine and season. Close the lid, bring up to high pressure and cook for 25 minutes. Reduce the pressure slowly. The squid should be very tender and the sauce thick and rich; if not, simmer uncovered to reduce.

2 Turn off the heat, leave to cool slightly, tip into a serving dish then drizzle with a little more olive oil and scatter with the coriander and orange zest.

PER SERVING (4) 352 kcals, protein 41g, carbs 12g, fat 8g, sat fat 2g, fibre 2g, sugar 7g, salt 0.8g

Steamed lemon tilapia with teriyaki sauce

If you can't get mirin for this recipe use white wine vinegar or rice vinegar instead and add an extra tablespoon of sugar.

TAKES 25 MINUTES ● SERVES 4

3 tbsp soy sauce
75ml/2½fl oz mirin
2 tbsp sugar
1 lemon, juice ½, ½ sliced into 4
250g/9oz basmati rice, rinsed in cold
   water
4 x 140g/5oz tilapia fillets
3cm/1¼in piece ginger, shredded
1 red chilli, deseeded and sliced
   (optional)
small bunch spring onions, sliced,
   to garnish
lemon slices, to serve

1 Pour the soy, mirin and sugar in a small pan with the lemon juice. Bring to the boil and simmer for 5 minutes until slightly syrupy. Remove and set aside.

2 Put the rice in a pressure cooker and cover with about 450ml/¾ pint water. Bring to high pressure, cook for 5 minutes, then slow-release the pressure – the rice should have absorbed about three-quarters of the water; if there isn't any liquid left add another 100ml/3½fl oz water.

3 Put the fish fillets on top of the rice. Sprinkle each with ginger, chilli and a slice of lemon. Season, cover with the lid, not for pressure but to steam for 6–8 minutes. The fish and rice should now be cooked through. Serve with the lemon slices, a drizzle of the sauce and sprinkled with the spring onions.

PER SERVING 409 kcals, protein 31g, carbs 70g, fat 3g, sat fat none, fibre 1g, sugar 12g, salt 2.23g

Japanese salmon & avocado rice

Pressure cookers are great for cooking rice – sushi rice is available from some supermarkets, but if you can't find it, simply use basmati.

TAKES 25 MINUTES ● SERVES 4

300g/10oz sushi rice

350g/12oz very fresh skinless salmon fillet

2 small ripe avocados, sliced

juice 1 lemon

4 tsp light soy sauce

4 tsp toasted sesame seeds

2 spring onions, thinly sliced

1 red chilli, deseeded and thinly sliced

small handful coriander leaves

1 Rinse the rice in a sieve until the water runs clear. Drain and put it in the pressure cooker with 450ml/¾ pint water. Close the lid, bring up to high pressure and cook for 3 minutes then reduce the pressure slowly.

2 While you are waiting for the pressure to drop, slice the salmon and arrange on a platter with the sliced avocado. Drizzle over the lemon juice and soy, making sure everything is evenly covered. Leave in the fridge to marinate for 10 minutes.

3 Carefully tip the juices from the salmon platter into the rice, then stir in with a little salt. Divide the rice among four bowls. Scatter the sesame seeds, spring onions, chilli and coriander over the salmon and avocado, then serve with the rice.

PER SERVING 519 kcals, protein 25g, carbs 59g, fat 22g, sat fat 3g, fibre 2g, sugar 1g, salt 1.02g

Spanish fish stew

Sustainable white fish or salmon fillets work best in this recipe, and you can also add 2 handfuls of mussels or clams 5 minutes before the end.

TAKES 35 MINUTES ● SERVES 4

handful flat-leaf parsley leaves, chopped
2 garlic cloves, finely chopped
zest and juice 1 lemon
3 tbsp olive oil, plus extra to drizzle
1 medium onion, finely sliced
500g/1lb 2oz floury potatoes, cut into small chunks
1 tsp paprika
pinch cayenne pepper
400g can chopped tomatoes
1 fish stock cube
200g/7oz raw peeled king prawns
½ x 410g can chickpeas, drained and rinsed
500g/1lb 2oz skinless fish fillets, cut into very large chunks
crusty bread, to serve (optional)

1 In a bowl, mix the parsley with half the garlic and the lemon zest, then set aside. Heat 2 tablespoons of oil in the pressure cooker. Add the onion and potatoes, then sweat for 5 minutes, until the onion has softened. Add the remaining oil, garlic and spices, then cook for 2 minutes more.
2 Pour over the lemon juice and sizzle for a moment. Add the tomatoes, ½ can water and crumble in the stock. Season with a little salt. Close the lid, bring up to high pressure and cook for 4 minutes until the potatoes are just cooked then fast-release the pressure.
3 Stir through the prawns and chickpeas, then nestle the fish chunks into the top of the stew. Re-cover the pan but not for pressure, then cook for about 8 minutes, stirring gently once or twice. When the fish is just cooked through, remove from the heat and scatter with the parsley mix. Serve with a drizzle of olive oil and some crusty bread, if you want.

PER SERVING 382 kcals, protein 39g, carbs 33g, fat 11g, sat fat 2g, fibre 5g, sugar 6g, salt 0.8g

Spiced-bulghar pilaf with fish

This flavoursome North African-inspired one-pot has the added advantage of being low in fat and superhealthy.

TAKES 45 MINUTES • SERVES 4

1 tbsp olive oil
2 onions, finely sliced
3 carrots, grated
2 tsp cumin seeds
2 tbsp harissa paste
200g/7oz bulghar wheat
6 dried apricots, chopped
700ml/1¼ pints weak chicken stock
   (we made using 1 stock cube)
200g/7oz baby leaf spinach
4 firm white fish fillets
4 thin lemon slices

1 Heat the oil in the pressure cooker. Tip in the onions and cook for 10 minutes until soft and golden. Add the carrots and cumin, and cook for 2 minutes more. Stir through the harissa, bulghar and apricots, and pour over the stock. Close the lid, bring up to high pressure and cook for 3 minutes then release the pressure slowly.

2 Add the spinach and stir through until just wilted. Arrange the fish fillets on top, pop a slice of lemon on each and season. Replace the lid, but not for pressure, and cook for 8–10 minutes more on a low heat so the bulghar wheat doesn't catch at the bottom – until the fish is cooked through and the bulghar wheat tender. Season with some freshly ground black pepper and serve.

PER SERVING 416 kcals, protein 37g, carbs 52g, fat 6g, sat fat 1g, fibre 7g, sugar 15g, salt 1g

Mussels steamed with cider & bacon

Mussels don't take long to cook anyway, but doing them in a pressure cooker locks in all their flavour and keeps them really succulent.

TAKES 15 MINUTES ● SERVES 2 GENEROUSLY AS A MAIN, 4 AS A STARTER

small knob butter

6 rashers bacon, chopped, or 140g/5oz piece, cut into small cubes

2 shallots, finely sliced

small bunch thyme, leaves stripped

1.5kg/3lb 5oz small mussels, scrubbed and bearded

glass cider (about 150ml/¼ pint)

2 tbsp crème fraîche (optional)

crusty bread, to serve

1 Heat the butter in the pressure cooker, then fry the bacon for 4 minutes, turning occasionally until it starts to crisp. Throw in the shallots and thyme leaves, then cook for 1 minute until softened. Whack the heat up to maximum, add the mussels to the pan, then pour over the cider. Close the lid, give the pan a good shake, bring up to high pressure and cook for 2 minutes, shaking the pan occasionally. Fast-release the pressure and all the mussels should have opened. Discard any that haven't.

2 Use a slotted spoon to scoop the mussels into bowls and put the pan back on the heat. Bring the juices to the boil and stir in the crème fraîche, if using. Pour the juice or the sauce over the mussels. Serve with hunks of crusty bread for mopping up the sauce.

PER SERVING (4) 367 kcals, protein 39g, carbs 8g, fat 18g, sat fat 6g, fibre none, sugar 2g, salt 4.45g

One-pot cabbage & beans with white fish

This cabbage stew is based on a peasant dish from south-west France called garbure, which is served with everything from duck to fish.

TAKES 45 MINUTES • SERVES 4

small knob butter

5 rashers smoked streaky bacon, chopped

1 onion, finely chopped

2 celery sticks, diced

2 carrots, diced

small bunch thyme

1 Savoy cabbage, shredded

4 tbsp white wine

300ml/½ pint chicken stock

410g can flageolet beans in water, drained and rinsed

FOR THE FISH

4 sustainable white fish fillets, such as hake (about 140g/5oz each), skin on

2 tbsp plain flour

2 tbsp olive oil

1 Heat the butter in the pressure cooker until starting to sizzle, add the bacon, then fry for a few minutes. Add the onion, celery and carrots, then gently cook for 8–10 minutes until softening, but not brown. Stir in the thyme and cabbage, then cook for a few minutes until the cabbage starts to wilt. Pour in the wine, simmer until evaporated, then add the stock and beans. Season, close the lid, bring up to high pressure and cook for 5 minutes then reduce the pressure slowly.

2 While you are waiting for the pressure to release, cook the fish. Season each fillet, then dust the skin with flour. Heat the oil in a frying pan. Fry the fish, skin-side down, for 4 minutes until crisp, then flip over and finish on the flesh side until cooked through. Serve each fish fillet on top of a pile of cabbage and beans.

PER SERVING 423 kcals, protein 42g, carbs 29g, fat 16g, sat fat 4g, fibre 10g, sugar 13g, salt 1.45g

Lemony prawn & pea risotto

Once you've seen how easy it is to make risotto in a pressure cooker you'll never make it the traditional way again.

TAKES 30 MINUTES • SERVES 4

2 tbsp olive oil
1 onion, chopped
300g/10oz risotto rice
150ml white wine
700ml/1¼ pint hot fish stock
400g bag peeled raw prawns,
    defrosted if frozen
200g/7oz frozen peas
1 red chilli deseeded, finely chopped
zest and juice 1 lemon

1 Heat half the olive oil in a pressure cooker, stir in the onion and sweat gently for 8–10 minutes until soft but not coloured, stirring occasionally. Stir the rice into the onion until completely coated in the oil, then stir continuously until the rice is shiny and the edges of the grain start to look transparent.

2 Pour in the wine and simmer until totally evaporated. Pour in the stock, close the lid, bring up to high pressure and cook for 5 minutes then release the pressure quickly. Put the pan back on a low heat and stir through the prawns and peas. Simmer gently until the prawns change colour. The risotto should be creamy. When you draw a wooden spoon through it, there should be a wake that holds for a few moments.

3 Stir through the chopped chilli, lemon juice and remaining olive oil. Let the risotto rest for a few minutes, then serve, topped with the lemon zest.

PER SERVING 411 kcals, protein 19g, carbs 66g, fat 7g, sat fat 1g, fibre 5g, sugar 3g, salt 1.8g

Chinese steamed bass with cabbage

Most pressure cookers come with a steamer attachment, and this supper for two takes full advantage of this piece of kit.

TAKES 25 MINUTES • SERVES 2

2 sea bass or other white fish fillets
   (about 100g/4oz each)
1 red or green chilli, deseeded and
   finely chopped
1 tsp finely chopped ginger
300g/10oz green cabbage, finely
   shredded
2 tsp sunflower oil
1 tsp sesame oil
2 garlic cloves, thinly sliced
2 tsp low-salt soy sauce

1 Sprinkle the fish with the chilli, ginger and a little salt. Pour 100ml/3½fl oz water into the pressure cooker then set up the steamer basket. Add the cabbage to the basket then put the fish fillets on top skin-side down. Close the lid, bring up to low pressure and cook for 4 minutes then reduce the pressure slowly.

2 Meanwhile, heat the oils in a small pan, add the garlic and quickly cook, stirring until lightly browned. Transfer the cabbage and fish to serving plates, sprinkle each with 1 teaspoon of the soy sauce, then pour over the garlicky oil.

PER SERVING 188 kcals, protein 23g, carbs 8g, fat 8g, sat fat 1g, fibre 4g, sugar 7g, salt 0.74g

Tender duck & pineapple red curry

This slow-cooked curry improves if made up to 2 days ahead, without the pineapple.
Simply add the pineapple before reheating.

TAKES 55 MINUTES • SERVES 4

4 duck legs
2 tbsp light soft brown sugar
4 tbsp Thai red curry paste
400ml can coconut milk
2 tbsp Thai fish sauce
6 kaffir lime leaves
1 small pineapple, peeled, cored and
  cut into chunks
1 red chilli, deseeded and finely sliced
  (optional)
small handful Thai basil leaves
  (optional)
steamed rice, to serve

1 Dry-fry the duck legs in batches in a pressure cooker on a low heat for a 10–15 minutes, turning once, until coloured all over. Remove the duck from the pan. Add the sugar to the fat in the pan and cook until caramelised, then add the curry paste and cook for few minutes. Stir in the coconut milk and ½ can water. Simmer, stirring until combined. Add the fish sauce and lime leaves.

2 Add the duck legs, close the lid, bring up to high pressure and cook for 30 minutes then release the pressure slowly. Lift the duck legs into another dish and remove the fat from the sauce. Put the pan back on the heat, add the pineapple and simmer for 2 minutes. Grill the duck if you want the skin crisp.

3 At the last moment, stir half the chilli and half the basil leaves, if using, through the sauce, and pour over the duck, then scatter with the rest of the chilli and basil. Serve with some rice.

PER SERVING 655 kcals, protein 48g, carbs 20g, fat 41g, sat fat 20g, fibre 2g, sugar 17g, salt 2.6g

Rabbit cacciatore

'Cacciatore' means hunter in Italian, and this preparation would have been applied to whatever meat the hunter had caught. Serve with polenta, mash or a flat pasta.

TAKES 1¾ HOURS ● SERVES 4

900g/2lb rabbit pieces
2 tbsp plain flour seasoned with salt
    and black pepper
3 tbsp olive oil
2 onions, chopped
3 garlic cloves, chopped
large bunch parsley, chopped
300ml/½ pint white wine
2 x 400g cans cherry tomatoes
about 20 large green olives
1 tbsp sugar

1 Toss the rabbit in the flour. Heat 1 tablespoon of the olive oil in the pressure cooker and brown the rabbit in three batches, adding another tablespoon of oil for each batch. Lift out all the rabbit and set aside. Add the onions and garlic to the pan then gently cook for 15 minutes until softened. Add most of the parsley and cook for a few minutes more. Return the rabbit to the pan and pour in the wine. Turn up the heat and bubble the wine; then stir in the tomatoes.

2 Close the lid, bring up to high pressure and cook for 30 minutes then slow-release the pressure. If the rabbbit is still tough, continue to simmer, uncovered, adding more water if needed, and the meat will become tender. When the meat is ready, throw in the olives and simmer for 5–10 minutes more. To serve, season with the sugar, salt and pepper, and scatter with the remaining parsley.

PER SERVING 591 kcals, protein 53g, carbs 23g, fat 30g, sat fat 7g, fibre 4g, sugar 17g, salt 3.25g

Chicken & white bean stew

This freezes really well, so why not make double and freeze half another time?

TAKES 50 MINUTES ● SERVES 4

2 tbsp sunflower oil
400g/14oz boneless skinless chicken
   thighs, trimmed and cut into chunks
1 onion, finely chopped
3 carrots, finely chopped
3 celery sticks, finely chopped
2 thyme sprigs or ½ tsp dried
1 bay leaf, fresh or dried
600ml/1 pint vegetable or chicken
   stock
2 x 400g cans haricot beans, drained
   and rinsed
small handful chopped parsley
crusty bread, to serve

1 Heat the oil in the pressure cooker, add the chicken, then fry until lightly browned. Add the vegetables, then fry for a few minutes more. Stir in the herbs and stock. Close the lid, bring up to high pressure and cook for 5 minutes then release the pressure slowly.

2 Stir the beans into the pan, then simmer, uncovered, for 5 minutes. If freezing, cool now then freeze for up to 1 month. Once ready to eat, stir in the parsley and serve with crusty bread.

PER SERVING 291 kcals, protein 30g, carbs 24g, fat 9g, sat fat 2g, fibre 11g, sugar 9g, salt 0.66g

Guinea fowl tagine with chickpeas, squash & apricots

It's all too easy to go down the traditional route with birds such as guinea fowl; however, they are just as suited to global dishes like this tagine.

TAKES 55 MINUTES • SERVES 6

3 tbsp olive oil
2 guinea fowl, jointed like a chicken
2 onions, roughly chopped
2 garlic cloves, chopped
1 small butternut squash or small pumpkin, peeled, deseeded and cut into large chunks
1 tbsp ras-el-hanout spice mix
1 tsp ground cumin
1 tsp ground coriander
½ tsp ground ginger
1 large cinnamon stick
small squeeze clear honey
large pinch saffron, soaked in 1 tbsp boiling water
juice 1 lemon
850ml/1½ pints chicken stock
400g can chickpeas, drained and rinsed
200g/7oz dried apricots
small bunch coriander
couscous or rice, to serve

1 Heat the oil in a pressure cooker. Season the guinea-fowl pieces and brown them – in batches, if necessary – then remove to a plate. Set aside.

2 Fry the onions in the cooker until softened, then add the garlic and squash or pumpkin, cooking for 1–2 minutes. Tip in the spices and cook for a few minutes before adding the honey, saffron and lemon juice. Pour in the chicken stock and the chickpeas.

3 Submerge the guinea-fowl pieces in the stock and add the apricots. Close the lid, bring up to high pressure and cook for 10 minutes then release the pressure slowly. The fowl and squash should both be tender, if not, simmer uncovered until they are. Stir through the coriander and serve with couscous or rice.

PER SERVING 591 kcals, protein 64g, carbs 31g, fat 22g, sat fat 5g, fibre 6g, sugar 20g, salt 1.1g

Chicken mole

If you're a fan of chilli con carne you'll love this sweet and spicy stew.

TAKES 1½ HOURS • SERVES 6

2 dried ancho chillies, available online
2 tbsp sunflower oil
8 bone-in chicken thighs, skin removed
2 onions, chopped
2 tsp ground cumin
1½ tsp ground cinnamon
3 garlic cloves, roughly chopped
50g/2oz raisins
2 tbsp smooth peanut butter
2 tbsp chipotle paste
400g can chopped tomatoes
25g/1oz dark chocolate (at least 70% cocoa solids)
1 small red onion, sliced into rings
juice 1 lime
150ml pot soured cream
cooked rice, to serve

1 Put the chillies in a bowl, cover with boiling water and leave to soften. Heat the oil in a pressure cooker then brown the chicken in batches. Add the onions and spices to the pan, and cook until soft.

2 Remove the chillies from the liquid, reserving the liquid, and discard the stalks and seeds. Whizz to a paste in a food processor with 4 tablespoons of the soaking liquid, the garlic and the raisins. Tip into the pan with the peanut butter, chipotle paste, tomatoes, 450ml/¾ pint water and the chicken; season. Close the lid, bring to high pressure and cook for 30 minutes then slow-release.

3 Remove the chicken. Shred the meat and discard the bones. Add the chicken and chocolate to the sauce, and cook, uncovered, for 30 minutes.

4 Put the red onion, lime juice and a pinch of salt in a bowl. Remove the pan from the heat, scatter with the red onion and serve with the rice and the soured cream.

PER SERVING 690 kcals, protein 28g, carbs 93g, fat 22g, sat fat 5g, fibre 3g, sugar 13g, salt 0.5g

Shredded duck, watercress & orange salad

Tender pressure-cooked duck meat is shredded and tossed through a fresh and crunchy salad – great for casual entertaining.

TAKES 1¼ HOURS • SERVES 4

2 duck legs
1 tsp five-spice powder
5 tbsp rice vinegar
5 tbsp soy sauce
2 big oranges, segmented, juice
    reserved
2 x 100g bag watercress
200g bag radishes, thinly sliced
140g pack white chicory, leaves
    separated
small bunch spring onions, sliced
    diagonally

1 Pat the duck legs dry with kitchen paper and rub in the five-spice and some seasoning. Pour the vinegar, soy, orange juice and 50ml/2fl oz water into a pressure cooker and add the duck. Close the lid, bring up to high pressure and cook for 30 minutes then slow-release the pressure.

2 Remove the meat and strain the liquid through a sieve, reserving the liquid. Let the duck cool until you can shred the meat from the bones and discard the skin and bones. Skim the fat from the liquid and set aside.

3 Meanwhile, gently toss together the orange segments, watercress, radishes, chicory and spring onions. Arrange the duck over the platter then pour over the reserved cooking liquid.

PER SERVING 307 kcals, protein 27g, carbs 23g, fat 16g, sat fat 4g, fibre 5g, sugar 18g, salt 3.8g

Chicken arrabbiata

The name actually means 'angry' because the chillies make it fiery, and, just like the pasta sauce, this dish is intended to pack quite a punch.

TAKES 1 HOUR 10 MINUTES

● **SERVES 6**

3 tbsp olive oil

2 medium onions, halved and sliced

1 garlic bulb, separated into cloves

2 red chillies, deseeded and sliced

350ml/12fl oz red wine

350ml/12fl oz chicken stock

600g/1lb 5oz tomatoes, finely chopped

3 tbsp tomato purée

2 tsp chopped thyme leaves

6 skinless chicken legs

chopped parsley leaves, to garnish (optional)

pasta or mash, to serve

1 Heat the olive oil in a pressure cooker. Add the onions and whole garlic cloves. Fry, stirring frequently, for 10 minutes, adding the chillies for the final minute.

2 Pour in the wine, turn up the heat and allow it to bubble for 1 minute to cook off the alcohol. Stir in the stock, tomatoes, tomato purée and thyme with some seasoning. Add the chicken legs, pushing them under the liquid. Close the lid, bring up to high pressure and cook for 25 minutes then reduce the pressure slowly.

3 Scoop out the chicken on to a plate, then simmer the sauce so it has reduced a little and thickened. Slip the chicken back in the sauce to heat through then scatter with parsley, if you like, and serve with pasta or mash.

PER SERVING 327 kcals, protein 35g, carbs 9g, fat 13g, sat fat 3g, fibre 3g, sugar 7g, salt 0.5g

Guinea fowl with lentils, sherry & bacon

This is one of those dishes that is really easy to throw together, but the end result has you brimming with pride.

TAKES 1¼ HOURS ● **SERVES 2–3**

1 tbsp olive oil, plus extra for drizzling
50g/2oz butter
1 small guinea fowl
100g/4oz smoked bacon lardons
1 carrot, finely chopped
1 onion, finely chopped
2 celery sticks, finely chopped
2 bay leaves
100g/4oz Puy lentils
100ml/3½fl oz dry sherry
225ml/8fl oz chicken stock
½ bunch tarragon
1 tbsp Dijon mustard

FOR THE SAUCE
100ml/3½fl oz double cream
juice ½ lemon
handful each tarragon leaves and
    parsley leaves, roughly chopped

1 Heat the oil and butter in a pressure cooker. Fry the guinea fowl gently for 10 minutes until browned, then remove.

2 Fry the bacon in the pressure cooker until starting to colour, then add the carrot, onion, celery and bay, and fry until softened. Stir in the lentils, pour over the sherry and chicken stock to cover, and add the tarragon. Nestle the bird back among the lentils, breast-side up. Close the lid, bring up to high pressure and cook for 20 minutes then release the pressure slowly.

3 To make the sauce, bring the cream and lemon juice to the boil and season. Remove from the heat, add the herbs, purée with a hand blender.

4 When the guinea fowl is ready, remove from the pan and stir the lentils. Add the mustard and a drizzle of oil, then transfer to a serving plate. Put the guinea fowl on top and serve with the sauce.

PER SERVING (3) 796 kcals, protein 72g, carbs 23g, fat 40g, sat fat 16g, fibre 5g, sugar 7g, salt 2.4g

Fragrant chicken curry with chickpeas

To keep this recipe as healthy as possible, there is no frying or oil involved.

TAKES 40 MINUTES • SERVES 4

2 onions, quartered

3 fat garlic cloves

3cm/1¼in piece ginger, peeled and
roughly chopped

2 tbsp medium curry powder

½ tsp turmeric powder

2 tsp paprika

1 fresh red chilli, deseeded and roughly
chopped

20g pack coriander

1 chicken stock cube

4 skinless boneless chicken breasts,
cubed

410g can chickpeas, drained and rinsed

natural low-fat yogurt, basmati rice,
naan bread or grilled poppadums,
to serve

1 Tip the onions, garlic, ginger, ground spices, chilli and half the coriander into a food processor. Add 1 teaspoon salt and blend to a purée. Tip the mixture into a pressure cooker and cook over a low heat for 10 minutes, stirring frequently.

2 Crumble in the stock cube, add 450ml/¾ pint boiling water and return to the boil. Add the chicken, stir, close the lid, bring up to high pressure and cook for 5 minutes then release the pressure slowly.

3 Chop the remaining coriander, reserve 2 tablespoons, then stir the remainder into the curry with the chickpeas. Heat through and divide among four bowls. Sprinkle with the reserved coriander and spoon over the yogurt, then serve with basmati rice, naan bread or poppadums.

PER SERVING 272 kcals, protein 39g, carbs 19g, fat 5g, sat fat 1g, fibre 5g, sugar none, salt 1.68g

Rabbit & chorizo rice

Think of this dish as a meatier version of paella. If you can't find paella rice, use risotto rice instead.

TAKES 50 MINUTES, PLUS
MARINATING • SERVES 6

1 rabbit, portioned and chopped into about 20 small pieces (ask your butcher to do this)
glass white wine (about 125ml/4fl oz)
1 tbsp olive oil, plus extra for frying
small bunch thyme
200g/7oz cooking chorizo, sliced
1 onion, chopped
3 garlic cloves, sliced
½ tsp smoked paprika
1 tbsp tomato purée
200g/7oz paella rice
450ml/16fl oz chicken stock
pinch saffron, soaked in 2 tbsp boiling water
200g/7oz frozen peas
bunch parsley, chopped, to garnish

1 Marinate the rabbit pieces in the wine, olive oil and thyme for 1 hour or overnight, if you can.

2 Drain the marinade from the rabbit, reserving the liquid. Heat the extra oil in a pressure cooker and sizzle the chorizo until crisp. Remove the chorizo and drain off the excess oil. Brown the rabbit pieces in two batches and set aside. Add the onion and garlic to the pressure cooker, cook until soft, then stir in the paprika and tomato purée. Stir in the rice, then pour over the reserved marinade, the stock and saffron.

3 Nestle the rabbit into the rice with the chorizo. Close the lid, cook on high for 8 minutes then release the pressure slowly. The rabbit should be tender and all the liquid absorbed. Stir through the frozen peas to defrost, then tip into a serving dish and scatter with parsley.

PER SERVING 397 kcals, protein 34g, carbs 33g, fat 13g, sat fat 5g, fibre 5g, sugar 4g, salt 1g

Barley, chicken & mushroom risotto

This low-fat version of risotto swaps the traditional rice for pearl barley, which makes it cheaper as well as healthier.

TAKES 45 MINUTES • SERVES 4

1 tbsp each butter and olive oil
2 large shallots, finely sliced
1 garlic clove, chopped
3 boneless skinless chicken breasts,
    cut into chunks
300g/10oz pearl barley
250ml/9fl oz white wine
400g/14oz mixed wild and chestnut
    mushrooms, left whole or halved if
    large
1 tbsp thyme leaves
1 litre/1¾ pints hot chicken stock
3 tbsp grated Parmesan
snipped chives and Parmesan shavings,
    to garnish (optional)

1 Heat the butter and oil in a pressure cooker. Sauté the shallots and garlic with some seasoning for 5 minutes, then stir in the chicken and cook for 2 minutes.

2 Add the barley and cook for 1 minute. Pour in the wine and stir until it is absorbed. Add the mushrooms and thyme, then pour over the stock. Close the lid, bring up to high pressure and cook for 20 minutes then release the pressure slowly. If a little watery, put back on the heat and simmer gently for a few minutes to reduce.

3 Stir in the grated Parmesan and serve immediately, with snipped chives and Parmesan shavings scattered over, if you like.

PER SERVING 564 kcals, protein 42g, carbs 61g, fat 12g, sat fat 5g, fibre 3g, sugar 3g, salt 1.1g

Duck au vin

Coq au vin is a delicious bistro regular; however, this version, made with duck, has an even richer flavour.

TAKES 1½ HOURS • SERVES 4

4 duck legs
4 tbsp plain flour
1 tbsp sunflower oil
3 carrots, chopped
1 onion, chopped
4 garlic cloves, roughly chopped
750ml red wine
tied bundle thyme and bay
140g/5oz smoked bacon lardoons
200g/7oz baby button mushrooms

1 Tip the duck into a large bowl and season; then toss in the flour. Heat the oil in a pressure cooker. Slowly brown the duck on all sides for 10 minutes in batches. Remove the duck to a plate, then add the carrots, onion and garlic to the pressure cooker, and cook for 5 minutes until just starting to colour.

2 Nestle the duck in the pan and pour over the wine. Add the herbs, season, then bring to the boil. Close the lid, cook for 30 minutes on high pressure then reduce the pressure slowly. Lift the duck into a container, strain the sauce into another and chill both. Once chilled, lift the fat off the sauce.

3 To serve, heat the cleaned pressure cooker and sizzle the lardons for 5 minutes. Turn up the heat, add the mushrooms and cook for 3–4 minutes. Return the duck and sauce to the pressure cooker. Simmer for 10 minutes until the duck is heated through.

PER SERVING 712 kcals, protein 55g, carbs 23g, fat 29g, sat fat 8g, fibre 3g, sugar 7g, salt 1.9g

Wild venison, field mushroom & ale pudding

Using a pressure cooker gives you tender meat, rich gravy and a light suet pastry.

TAKES 2½ HOURS, PLUS CHILLING

● **SERVES 4–6**

FOR THE PASTRY

450g/1lb self-raising flour

1tsp salt

225g/8oz shredded beef suet

FOR THE FILLING

2 large onions, thinly sliced

1 tbsp each butter and vegetable oil,
    plus extra oil

8 garlic cloves, thinly sliced

4 large field mushrooms, stems
    removed

500g/1lb 2oz diced venison shoulder

1 tbsp plain flour, seasoned with salt
    and pepper

1 tsp tomato purée

200ml/7fl oz brown ale

1 tsp sugar

4 thyme sprigs, leaves picked

1 Sift the salt and the flour and stir in the suet. Add 300ml/½ pint cold water and work into a dough. Cover and chill.

2 Fry the onions and garlic in the butter and oil until soft then remove. Fry the mushrooms in more oil then remove. Toss the venison in the flour and fry in batches. Mix in the purée, ale, sugar and thyme.

3 Butter a 1.4-litre pudding basin. Roll out the pastry and use to line the sides of the basin. Trim, leaving an overhang. Roll the trimmings and cut out a lid wider than the the basin. Put the mushrooms around the sides, then fill with meat and juices.

4 Put the lid on top and seal. Make a double layer of buttered foil and baking paper, and pleat it. Scrunch over the pudding, foil-side up, then tie with string under the rim. Sit the pudding on a trivet in a pressure cooker. Add 500ml/18fl oz boiling water. Cover with a lid, not for pressure. Steam for 20 minutes then cook for 1½ hours on low then slow-release the pressure. Turn out onto a plate.

PER SERVING(6) 777 kcals, protein 28g, carbs 71g fat 44g, sat fat 18g, fibre 4g, sugar 7g, salt 2g

One-pot chicken chasseur

A French classic that makes the most of cheap chicken legs but is still special enough to serve to friends.

TAKES 1¼ HOURS ● SERVES 4

1 tsp olive oil
25g/1oz butter
4 chicken legs
1 onion, chopped
2 garlic cloves, crushed
200g pack small button or chestnut
　mushrooms
225ml/8fl oz red wine
2 tbsp tomato purée
2 thyme sprigs
500ml/18fl oz chicken stock
fried cabbage, to serve (optional)

1 Heat the oil and half the butter in a pressure cooker. Season the chicken, then fry for about 5 minutes on each side until golden brown. Remove the chicken to a plate.

2 Melt the rest of the butter in the cooker. Add the onion, then fry for about 5 minutes until soft. Add the garlic, cook for about 1 minute, add the mushrooms, cook for 2 minutes, then add the wine. Stir in the tomato purée, let the liquid bubble and reduce for about 5 minutes, then stir in the thyme and pour over the stock. Slip the chicken back into the pan, close the lid, bring up to high pressure and cook for 20 minutes then release the pressure slowly.

3 Remove the chicken from the pan and keep warm. Rapidly boil down the sauce for 10 minutes or so until it is syrupy and the flavour has concentrated. Put the chicken legs back into the sauce and serve with fried cabbage, if you like.

PER SERVING 439 kcals, protein 35g, carbs 7g, fat 28g, sat fat 10g, fibre 2g, sugar 6g, salt 1.11g

Braised rabbit ragout

It's a mystery why we don't eat more wild rabbit in the UK. The flavour is often compared to chicken, yet the meat is leaner and always free-range.

TAKES 1¾ HOURS ● SERVES 5

2 tbsp olive oil
1 wild rabbit, jointed (ask your butcher to do this for you)
4 rashers smoked streaky bacon, chopped
1 small red onion, finely chopped
1 carrot, finely chopped
3 garlic cloves, crushed
2 rosemary sprigs, leaves picked and chopped
1 tbsp tomato purée
150ml/¼ pint white or rosé wine
500ml/18fl oz chicken stock
zest ½ orange
1 tbsp Dijon mustard
100ml/3½fl oz double cream
small bunch flat-leaf parsley, chopped, plus a few leaves picked to garnish
grated Parmesan, to garnish
cooked pappardelle pasta, to serve

1 Heat the oil in a pressure cooker. Add the rabbit, brown on all sides, then remove from the pan and set aside.

2 Add the bacon, onion and carrot to the pan, and cook for 10 minutes until soft. Add the garlic, rosemary and tomato purée, stir for 1–2 minutes, then pour in the wine and chicken stock.

3 Return the rabbit to the pan and season. Close the lid, bring to high pressure and cook for 30 minutes then release the pressure slowly.

4 Remove the rabbit from the pan and shred the meat. Be careful to remove all small bones. Meanwhile, boil the liquid in the pan for 5 minutes until reduced by half. Add the shredded meat and reduce the heat to low.

5 Stir half the orange zest, the mustard, cream and parsley into the rabbit sauce. Serve over pappardelle pasta with grated Parmesan, extra parsley leaves and the remaining orange zest scattered over.

PER SERVING 633 kcals, protein 40g, carbs 57g, fat 25g, sat fat 11g, fibre 2g, sugar 6g, salt 1.4g

Moroccan-style chicken with lentils

Serve this rich chicken dish with rice or couscous and a generous dollop of yogurt.

TAKES 55 MINUTES • SERVES 4

2 tbsp olive oil
8 boneless skinless chicken thighs
2 garlic cloves, crushed
1 tbsp ground cumin
1 tbsp ground coriander seeds
1 tbsp sweet paprika
1 large onion, finely sliced
50g/2oz red split lentils
400g can chopped tomatoes
1 tbsp tomato ketchup
700ml/1¼ pints chicken stock
1 cinnamon stick
200g/7oz whole dried apricots
handful mint leaves, to garnish
  (optional)
dollop of yogurt, to serve (optional)
couscous or rice, to serve

1 Rub 1 tablespoon of the olive oil into the chicken thighs. Mix the garlic, cumin, coriander and paprika together, then rub all over the chicken thighs on both sides.

2 Heat a pressure cooker, add the chicken thighs and cook over a medium heat for 5 minutes until golden on both sides. You might need to do this in two batches. Remove the chicken to a plate. Turn down the heat, add the remaining oil and fry the onion for 5 minutes until softened.

3 Stir in the rest of the ingredients, apart from the mint and rice, put the chicken thighs on top and pour in any juices. Close the lid, bring up to high pressure and cook for 15 minutes then release the pressure slowly. Scatter with mint leaves and spoon on a dollop of yogurt, if using, and serve with couscous or rice.

PER SERVING 461 kcals, protein 48g, carbs 40g, fat 13g, sat fat 3g, fibre 6g, sugar 1g, salt 1.45g

Duck legs in port

You wouldn't normally go to the bother of slow-cooking for two people, but doing so in a pressure cooker makes it easy and worthwhile.

TAKES 1 HOUR 20 MINUTES

● **SERVES 2**

2 duck legs
2 carrots, roughly chopped
1 small onion, roughly chopped
1 tbsp plain flour
1 bay leaf
1 star anise
2 whole cloves
2 strips orange skin (with a potato peeler)
150ml/¼ pint port
500ml/18fl oz chicken stock
seasonal vegetables, to serve

1 Put the duck legs in a pressure cooker set over a medium heat. Brown all over, then remove from the pan to a plate. Pour off all but 1 tablespoon of the fat; then add the carrots and onion to the pan and cook for 5–10 minutes or until starting to caramelise. Stir in the flour and cook for 1 minute more. Return the duck to the pan along with the remaining ingredients. Close the lid, bring up to high pressure and cook for 30 minutes then release the pressure slowly.

2 Remove the duck legs from the pan, strain the cooking liquid into a jug then pour back into the pan and bring to a rapid boil. Reduce the sauce by half until thickened and glossy. Return the duck legs to the sauce to heat through. Put a duck leg on each plate with a little sauce spooned over the top and serve with seasonal vegetables.

PER SERVING 841 kcals, protein 39g, carbs 37g, fat 50g, sat fat 27g, fibre 6g, sugar 22g, salt 1.4g

Spicy chicken & bean stew

A low-fat stew that is comforting and healthy but won't leave anyone hungry.

TAKES 45 MINUTES • SERVES 6

1.25kg/2lb 12oz chicken thighs and
  drumsticks
1 tbsp olive oil
2 onions, sliced
1 garlic clove, crushed
2 red chillies, deseeded and chopped
250g/9oz frozen peppers, defrosted
400g can chopped tomatoes
420g can kidney beans in chilli sauce
400g can butter beans, drained and
  rinsed
400ml/14fl oz hot chicken stock
small bunch coriander, chopped
150ml pot soured cream
crusty bread, to serve

1 Pull the skin off the chicken and discard. Heat the oil in a pressure cooker and brown the chicken all over, then remove to a plate with a slotted spoon. Tip in the onions, garlic and chillies, then fry for 5 minutes until starting to soften and turn golden.

2 Add the peppers, tomatoes, beans and hot stock. Put the chicken on top, close the lid, bring up to high pressure and cook for 15 minutes then release the pressure quickly. The chicken should be cooked through and tender. Stir through the coriander, tip into a serving dish and serve with dollops of the soured cream and some crusty bread on the side.

PER SERVING 348 kcals, protein 40g, carbs 23g, fat 10g, sat fat 3g, fibre 8g, sugar 11g, salt 1.3g

Gamekeeper's pie

The stew part of this recipe is cooked in a pressure cooker, and then it's turned into a comforting game version of shepherd's pie.

TAKES 2 HOURS 10 MINUTES

● **SERVES 6**

50g/2oz butter
1 tbsp olive oil
1 large onion, chopped
2 carrots, chopped
1kg/2lb 4oz mixed game meat (partridge, pigeon, pheasant, rabbit and hare all work well), deboned and cut into 2.5cm/1in pieces
2 tbsp plain flour
1 tbsp tomato purée
150ml/¼ pint red wine
500ml/18fl oz chicken or beef stock
1 tbsp Worcestershire sauce
1 bay leaf
4 tsp thyme leaves, chopped
400g/14oz potatoes, cut into chunks
600g/1lb 5oz mixed root veg (use parsnips, celeriac, swede or turnips), cut into chunks
2 tbsp milk

1 Heat half the butter and the oil in a pressure cooker, add the onion and carrots, and cook for about 10 minutes until soft. Add the game, then turn and cook for 10 minutes until nicely browned.

2 Stir the flour and tomato purée into the meat, cook for 1 minute, then add the wine, stock, Worcestershire sauce, bay leaf and 3 teaspoons of the thyme. Close the lid, bring up to high pressure and cook for 30 minutes, then release the pressure quickly. The meat should be tender and the sauce thickened.

3 Put the potatoes and veg in a large pan, cover with water, bring to the boil and cook for 20 minutes until tender. Drain, leave for 5 minutes, then mash with seasoning, milk and the remaining butter.

4 Heat oven to 220C/200C fan/gas 7. Tip the meat into an ovenproof dish and spoon on the mash. Sprinkle with the remaining thyme and bake for 45 minutes until golden and the sauce is bubbling.

PER SERVING 435 kcals, protein 26g, carbs 31g, fat 21g, sat fat 8g, fibre 9g, sugar 11g, salt 1.1g

Pot-roasted pheasant

This pressure-cooker version of a classic pot roast works equally well with partridge, guinea fowl or chicken.

TAKES 1 HOUR • SERVES 4

2 small pheasants, tied (ask your
    butcher to do this)
1 tbsp plain flour, well seasoned
50ml/2fl oz vegetable oil
2 rashers smoked streaky bacon, thinly
    sliced
8 shallots, peeled and left whole
2 carrots, peeled and quartered
    lengthways
2 parsnips, peeled and quartered
    lengthways
1 garlic clove, peeled and crushed
1 thyme sprig
2 bay leaves
100ml/3½fl oz Marsala or sweet sherry
50ml/2fl oz red wine
200ml/7fl oz chicken stock
1 tsp caster sugar

1 Dust the pheasants with the flour, then heat the oil in a pressure cooker. Brown the pheasants all over, then remove to a plate.

2 In the same pan, fry the bacon, vegetables, garlic and herbs with 1 tablespoon of the dusting flour for 5 minutes, until the vegetables start to colour. Put the pheasants and any resting juices back in the dish, pour on the Marsala, wine and stock, and add the sugar. Close the lid, bring up to high pressure and cook for 20–25 minutes then release the pressure slowly.

3 Lift out the pheasants with the veg. Simmer the sauce in the uncovered pan until reduced and thickened and pour over the birds to serve.

PER SERVING 565 kcals, protein 45g, carbs 19g, fat 30g, sat fat 7g, fibre 5g, sugar 12g, salt 0.95g

Mustard chicken with winter vegetables

This is a great way to make a chicken go further. Herby potatoes make a healthy accompaniment to mop up the delicious juices.

TAKES 1½ HOURS ● **SERVES 6**

1 chicken (about 1.8kg/4lb)
2 onions
6 celery sticks
6 carrots
2 bay leaves
2 thyme sprigs
1 tsp black peppercorns
50g/2oz butter
100g/4oz smoked bacon lardons
3 small turnips, peeled and cut into
    wedges
1 tbsp plain flour
850ml/1½ pints stock
2 tbsp wholegrain mustard
3 rounded tbsp crème fraîche
good handful parsley leaves, chopped,
    to garnish

1 Put the chicken in a pressure cooker. Halve 1 each of the onions, celery sticks and carrots. Add to the pot with the herbs and black peppercorns. Add water to come halfway up the chicken. Close the lid and cook for 30 minutes on high then release the pressure slowly. Cool, remove the chicken to a dish and strain the stock.
2 When cool enough, strip off the chicken meat and tear into pieces.
3 Chop the remaining onion, celery and carrot into thick slices. Heat the butter in the pressure cooker, add the onion and lardons, then gently fry until just starting to brown. Add the remaining veg, then fry for 2 minutes. Stir in the flour, then cook for 1 minute. Slowly add the stock to the pan, stirring. Close the lid, cook for 3 minutes on high then release the pressure quickly.
4 Return the chicken to the pan with the mustard and crème fraîche. Simmer and stir. Season and sprinkle with parsley.

PER SERVING 920 kcals, protein 71g, carbs 20g, fat 62g, sat fat 23g, fibre 6g, sugar 14g, salt 3.06g

Wild rabbit with rosemary, olive oil & garlic

The large amount of good olive oil involved in this recipe works to keep the rabbit meltingly soft – it's the same as cooking confit-style.

TAKES 1 HOUR 40 MINUTES
- **SERVES 6**

2 wild rabbits, jointed into legs, shoulders and half saddles (ask your butcher to do this for you)
50g/2oz plain flour, seasoned
125ml/4fl oz extra virgin olive oil
10 rosemary sprigs
20 garlic cloves, unpeeled
300ml/½ pint white wine
sauteéd potatoes or creamy mash and buttered greens, to serve

1 Toss the rabbit pieces in the flour and tap off the excess. Heat a few tablespoons of the oil in a pressure cooker then brown the pieces in batches, if necessary.

2 When they are lovely and golden brown, fit all the pieces back in the pan, throw in the rosemary, garlic and all of the olive oil. Add the wine and mix well. Bring the mixture up to the boil, close the lid, bring to low pressure and cook for 1 hour then release the pressure slowly. After this time the sauce should be thickened and the rabbit should come away from the bones really easily. Season and serve the whole lot with sauteéd potatoes or creamy mash and buttered greens.

PER SERVING 423 kcals, protein 38g, carbs 10g, fat 22g, sat fat 5g, fibre 1g, sugar 2g, salt 0.2g

Easy chicken casserole

A light, quick and good-value chicken and vegetable stew that can be whipped up and be on the table in less than an hour.

TAKES 40 MINUTES • SERVES 4

1 tbsp olive oil

8 bone-in chicken thighs, skin pulled off
and discarded

5 spring onions, sliced, white and green
parts separated

2 tbsp plain flour

2 chicken stock cubes

2 large carrots, cut into batons (no
need to peel)

400g/14oz new potatoes, halved if
large

200g/7oz frozen peas

1 tbsp grainy mustard

small handful fresh soft herbs, such as
parsley, chives, dill or tarragon,
chopped/ snipped

1 Put the kettle on. Heat the oil in a pressure cooker and fry the thighs to brown quickly. Stir in the white parts of the spring onion with the flour and stock cubes until the flour disappears, then gradually stir in 500ml/18fl oz hot water from the kettle. Throw in the carrots and potatoes, and bring to a simmer. Close the lid, bring up to high pressure and cook for 5 minutes then release the pressure slowly.

2 Take off the lid then throw in the peas and simmer for another 5 minutes. Season, stir in the mustard, green spring-onion bits, herbs and some seasoning.

PER SERVING 386 kcals, protein 43g, carbs 32g, fat 10g, sat fat 2g, fibre 6g, sugar 8g, salt 2.1g

Sticky baked gammon

Using a pressure cooker to cook the gammon before it is baked easily shaves a few hours off the whole process.

TAKES 2¼ HOURS ● **SERVES 10**

3–4kg/6lb 8oz–8lb 8oz gammon (doesn't need to be 1 piece, just make up the weight with smaller joints)
1 litre/1¾ pints pineapple juice
1 tbsp ground allspice
100g/4oz black treacle
100g/4oz ginger, roughly chopped
3 tbsp each tomato ketchup, sweet chilli sauce and clear honey

1 Put the gammon in a pressure cooker. Reserve 150ml/¼ pint of the pineapple juice and pour the rest over the gammon. Close the lid, bring up to high pressure and cook for 1 hour then release the pressure slowly.

2 Remove the gammon and pour off the cooking liquid. Cut away the rind and most of the fat, leaving just a thin layer of fat on the joint or joints.

3 Whizz the reserved pineapple juice, allspice, treacle, ginger, ketchup, sweet chilli and honey together to combine to a purée. Spoon all over the gammon and set aside until ready to cook.

4 Heat oven to 200C/180C fan/gas 6. Roast for 30 minutes until hot and sticky, then loosely break into large chunks to serve.

PER SERVING 593 kcals, protein 61g, carbs 15g, fat 32g, sat fat 11g, fibre none, sugar 14g, salt 8.3g

Boston baked beans

Haricot beans take very well to the sweetly spiced flavours of this dish. This is perfect family fare – kids will love it.

TAKES 2 HOURS, PLUS SOAKING
● **SERVES 6**

500g pack dried haricot beans
2 onions, roughly chopped
2 celery sticks, roughly chopped
2 carrots, roughly chopped
2 tbsp Dijon mustard
2 tbsp light muscovado sugar
½ tbsp black treacle or molasses
2 tbsp tomato purée
800g/1lb 12oz piece belly pork
handful parsley, roughly chopped,
　　to garnish

1 Soak the beans in a large bowl of cold water for at least 4 hours or overnight. Drain and rinse the beans, and put in the pressure cooker with 1.5 litres/2½ pints water. Boil for 10 minutes, skimming off any scum that appears on the surface.
2 Add the onions, celery, carrots, Dijon mustard, sugar, treacle or molasses and tomato purée. Stir until everything is well mixed, then bury the piece of pork among the beans. Close the lid, bring up to high pressure and cook for 1 hour then release the pressure slowly.
3 Take the pork out of the pot. Cut into large chunks and serve with the beans, sprinkled with parsley.

PER SERVING 615 kcals, protein 43g, carbs 54g, fat 27g, sat fat 10g, fibre 16g, sugar 14g, salt 0.8g

Sausage & lentil one-pot

If you can find Italian-style sausages flavoured with fennel for this recipe then all the better, but any good-quality pork sausages will work.

TAKES 55 MINUTES ● SERVES 4

1 tbsp olive oil
8 sausages
1 onion, finely chopped
1 garlic clove, crushed
1 red pepper, deseeded and sliced
250g/9oz lentils (we used Puy lentils)
125ml/4fl oz red wine (or use extra
    stock)
150ml/¼ pint vegetable stock
crusty bread, to serve

1 Heat half the oil in a pressure cooker, uncovered, and fry the sausages until browned, then remove to a plate. Tip in the remaining oil, onion, garlic and red pepper, and cook for 5 minutes until softened. Add the lentils and sausages to the pan with the wine and bring up to the boil, allow to bubble for a minute then pour over the stock.

2 Close the lid, bring up to high pressure and cook for 15 minutes, then reduce the pressure quickly. The lentils should now have softened and the sausages will be cooked through. Serve with plenty of crusty bread.

PER SERVING 556 kcals, protein 28g, carbs 45g, fat 29g, sat fat 9g, fibre 8g, sugar 8g, salt 2.42g

Fruity lamb tagine

This satisfying and superhealthy one-pot would normally take a long time to cook in the oven, but not with a pressure cooker.

TAKES 1¼ HOURS • SERVES 4

2 tbsp olive oil
500g/1lb 2oz lean diced lamb
1 large onion, roughly chopped
2 large carrots, quartered lengthways
    and cut into chunks
2 garlic cloves, finely chopped
2 tbsp ras-el-hanout spice mix
400g can chopped tomatoes
400g can chickpeas, drained and rinsed
200g/7oz dried apricots
600ml/1 pint chicken stock
120g pack pomegranate seeds
2 large handfuls coriander leaves,
    roughly chopped
couscous or rice, to serve

1 Heat the oil in a pressure cooker and brown the lamb on all sides. Scoop the lamb out on to a plate, then add the onion and carrots, and cook for 2–3 minutes until golden. Add the garlic and cook for 1 minute more. Stir in the spices and tomatoes, and season. Tip the lamb back in with the chickpeas and apricots.

2 Pour over the stock, stir and bring to a simmer. Close the lid, bring up to high pressure and cook for 20 minutes, then release the pressure slowly. When ready, leave the tagine to rest so it's not piping hot, then serve scattered with the pomegranate seeds and coriander, with couscous or rice alongside.

PER SERVING 497 kcals, protein 40g, carbs 46g, fat 18g, sat fat 5g, fibre 12g, sugar 32g, salt 1.37g

Red braised ginger-pork belly

Chinese black vinegar isn't as sour as other vinegars – it has a malty, sweet taste, and it is worth a search for it to make this recipe truly authentic.

TAKES 1¼ HOURS, PLUS MARINATING
● **SERVES 6**

2.5kg/5lb 8oz pork belly, rind removed, cut into 5cm/2in pieces
1 tbsp dark soy sauce
200ml/7fl oz Shaohsing rice wine
2 tbsp vegetable oil
2 garlic cloves, thinly sliced
thumb-sized piece ginger, cut into matchsticks
pinch chilli flakes
100ml/3½fl oz Chinese black vinegar
140g/5oz soft brown sugar
700ml/1¼ pints vegetable stock
2 red chillies, sliced and soaked in rice wine vinegar for 1 hour, then drained
toasted sesame seeds and sliced spring onions, to garnish
steamed white rice, to serve

1 Toss the pork with the soy and 1 tablespoon of the rice wine. Leave to marinate for at least 1 hour or, even better, overnight in the fridge.

2 Heat some of the oil in a pressure cooker. Brown the meat, in batches, and set aside. Add a little more oil and cook the garlic, ginger and chilli for 2–3 minutes until golden.

3 Pour the vinegar, remaining rice wine, the sugar and stock into the pan and bring to the boil. Add the pork, close the lid, bring up to high pressure and cook for 20 minutes then release the pressure slowly. Remove the lid, put the pan on a high heat and let the liquid boil and reduce for about 20 minutes until thick and syrupy. Tip into a serving dish and scatter with the sliced chillies, spring onions and sesame seeds, and serve with rice.

PER SERVING 925 kcals, protein 69g, carbs 27g, fat 61g, sat fat 20g, fibre 1g, sugar 25g, salt 1.7g

Beef & stout stew with carrots

Sweet, slow-cooked melty carrots are one of the best bits about a rustic stew, so here we've upped the quantity so there are lots to go round.

TAKES 1 HOUR 20 MINUTES
- **SERVES 4**

2 tbsp vegetable oil
1kg/2lb 4oz stewing beef, cut into large chunks
1 onion, roughly chopped
10 carrots, cut into large chunks
2 tbsp plain flour
500ml can brown stout, such as Guinness
1 beef stock cube
pinch sugar
3 bay leaves
big thyme sprig
creamy parsnip mash, to serve

1 Heat the oil in a pressure cooker, brown the meat really well in batches, then remove to a plate. Add the onion and carrots to the pan, give them a good browning, then scatter over the flour and stir. Tip the meat and any juices back into the pan and give it all a good stir. Pour over the stout and crumble in the stock cube. Season the stew with some salt, black pepper and the pinch of sugar. Tuck in the herbs and bring everything to a simmer.

2 Close the lid, bring up to high pressure and cook for 30 minutes then release the pressure slowly. The stew can now be chilled and frozen for up to 3 months – defrost completely before reheating until piping hot. Or leave the stew to settle a little, then serve with parsnip mash.

PER SERVING 562 kcals, protein 58g, carbs 26g, fat 23g, sat fat 8g, fibre 6g, sugar 20g, salt 1.5g

Fragrant pork & rice one-pot

Using sausage meat to make meatballs is a clever time-saving trick, and they work well in a tomato sauce served with pasta.

TAKES 45 MINUTES • SERVES 4

4–6 good-quality pork sausages
1 tbsp olive oil
½ onion, finely chopped
2 garlic cloves, crushed
2 tsp each ground cumin and coriander
140g/5oz long grain rice
850ml/1½ pints vegetable stock
400g can chopped tomatoes
½ small bunch coriander, leaves picked
crusty bread, to serve

1 Split the sausage skins, squeeze out the meat, then roll it into small meatballs each about the size of a large olive. Heat the oil in a pressure cooker then brown the meatballs well on all sides until cooked – you might need to do this in batches. Remove the meatballs to a plate.

2 Add the onion and garlic to the pan and cook for 5 minutes until soft. Stir in the spices and rice, and cook for another minute. Pour in the stock and tomatoes. Bring to a simmer, scraping up any sausagey bits from the bottom of the pan. Close the lid, bring up to high pressure and cook for 5 minutes then release the pressure slowly. Stir in the meatballs with some seasoning. Ladle into bowls, scatter with coriander and serve with crusty bread.

PER SERVING 408 kcals, protein 17g, carbs 43g, fat 20g, sat fat 5g, fibre 2g, sugar 6g, salt 1.56g

Braised oxtail with basil dumplings

Oxtail is transformed in the pressure cooker from a tough cut to soft, melting meat with a glistening sauce that goes really well with these basil dumplings.

TAKES 1¾ HOURS ● SERVES 6

2 oxtails, jointed and cut into pieces

2 tbsp plain flour

4 tbsp sunflower oil, plus extra to drizzle

2 onions, chopped

3 carrots, cut into small chunks

2 celery sticks, cut into small chunks

2 garlic cloves, chopped

2 tbsp tomato purée

bay leaves and thyme sprigs, tied together

75cl bottle full-bodied red wine

1 beef stock cube

basil leaves, to garnish

FOR THE DUMPLINGS

300g/10oz self-raising flour, plus extra for rolling

bunch basil, leaves removed

85g/3oz butter

3 egg whites

1 Coat the oxtails in the flour. Heat the oil in a pressure cooker. Brown the meat in batches then remove. Add the veg and garlic, and fry until starting to colour. Stir in the tomato purée and herbs. Tip the meat back into the pan, pour over the wine, then crumble in the stock cube. Season, close the lid, cook for 50 minutes on high then release the pressure slowly.

2 For the dumplings, blitz the flour, basil and a pinch of salt in a food processor. Add the butter and blitz until it resembles breadcrumbs. Slowly add the egg whites until everything comes together. On a floured surface, roll the dumplings into walnut-sized balls then cover.

3 Boil a large pan of salted water, lower in the dumplings and simmer for 15 minutes. Remove with a slotted spoon. Gently reheat the meat in the sauce.

4 Serve a few chunks of meat with a few dumplings, drizzled with olive oil and a scattering of basil leaves.

PER SERVING 812 kcals, protein 53g, carbs 50g, fat 41g, sat fat 17g, fibre 4g, sugar 8g, salt 2.08g

Vietnamese lamb shanks with sweet potatoes

This freezes well for up to 3 months. Defrost completely before heating on the hob, and add the lime juice and herbs just before serving.

TAKES 1¾ HOURS ● SERVES 4

2 tbsp sunflower oil

4 lamb shanks

2 onions, halved and cut into half
    moons

2 tbsp finely chopped ginger

3 garlic cloves, finely sliced

2 red chillies, deseeded, 1 chopped,
    1 thinly sliced

1 tbsp soft brown sugar, plus 1 tsp

3 star anise

2 lemongrass stalks, tough outer leaves
    removed, then bruised

500ml/18 fl oz lamb stock

1½ tbsp tomato purée

4 small sweet potatoes, peeled and cut
    into chunks

2 tbsp Thai fish sauce

juice 2 limes

big handful mint leaves, chopped, and
    handful basil leaves, torn, to garnish

1 Heat 1 tablespoon of oil in a pressure cooker, season the shanks, then brown them two at a time on all sides, adding the remaining oil for the second batch. Remove the lamb and add the onions. Fry them quite briskly for about 30 seconds, then add the ginger, garlic and chopped chilli, then turn the heat down and cook for 1 minute. Add the sugar, stir, then add the star anise, lemongrass, stock, purée and some seasoning. Close the lid, bring up to high pressure and cook for 30 minutes, then release the pressure slowly.

2 Add the sweet potatoes, close the lid, bring up to high pressure and cook for 15 minutes more, then release the pressure quickly. The lamb should be completely tender and almost falling off the bones. Stir in the fish sauce, lime juice and extra sugar just to lift the flavour, then scatter with the mint, basil and sliced chilli to serve.

PER SERVING 700 kcals, protein 64g, carbs 35g, fat 31g, sat fat 11g, fibre 5g, sugar 20g, salt 2g

Keema with peas

Traditionally this Gujarati-style curry uses cassia leaves and other individual spices; however, garam masala plus turmeric will give you as good a result.

TAKES 40 MINUTES ● SERVES 4

1 large onion, chopped
2 garlic cloves, chopped
5cm/2in piece ginger, grated
2 green chillies
3 tbsp vegetable oil
500g/1lb 2oz minced lamb
2 tbsp garam masala
2 tsp turmeric powder
½ x 400g can chopped tomatoes
   (freeze the rest)
2 tbsp natural yogurt, plus extra to
   serve
200g/7oz defrosted frozen peas or
   cooked fresh peas
small bunch coriander leaves, chopped
Indian breads or poppadums and
   chutney, to serve

1 Chop the onion, garlic, ginger and chillies together in a food processor. Heat the oil in a pressure cooker and fry the onion mixture until it becomes very fragrant. Add the mince and fry until it begins to brown, stirring to break up any lumps.

2 Add the spices and fry for 1 minute. Add the tomatoes and bring to a simmer, cook for 1 minute, then stir in the yogurt, some salt and a good grind of black pepper. Add a splash of water, close the lid, bring up to high pressure and cook for 15 minutes, then release the pressure quickly, remove the lid and put on a low heat. Add the peas and cook for 5 minutes, then stir in the coriander.

3 Serve the keema with Indian breads or poppadums, chutney and some more yogurt.

PER SERVING 427 kcals, protein 30g, carbs 17g, fat 27g, sat fat 10g, fibre 4g, sugar 6g, salt 0.33g

Irish stew

The trick with this classic one-pot is to use a cheap cut of meat. Middle neck (neck fillets) or scrag end are both great for braising.

TAKES 1 HOUR 25 MINUTES
- **SERVES 6**

1 tbsp sunflower oil
200g/7oz smoked streaky bacon, preferably in one piece, skinned and cut into chunks
900g/2lb stewing lamb, cut into large chunks
5 medium onions, sliced
5 carrots, sliced into chunks
3 bay leaves
small bunch thyme
100g/4oz pearl barley
850ml/1½ pints lamb stock
6 medium potatoes, cut into chunks
small knob butter
3 spring onions, finely sliced

1 Heat the oil in a pressure cooker. Sizzle the bacon for 4 minutes until crisp. Turn up the heat, then cook the lamb for 6 minutes until brown. Remove the meats with a slotted spoon. Add the onions, carrots and herbs to the pan, then cook for about 5 minutes until soft.

2 Return the meat to the pan, stir in the pearl barley and pour over the stock. Close the lid, bring up to high pressure and cook for 30 minutes then release the pressure quickly.

3 Sit the chunks of potato on top of the stew, close the lid again, bring up to high pressure and cook for 5 minutes more, then release the pressure slowly. Dot the potatoes with butter, scatter with the spring onions and serve scooped straight from the dish.

PER SERVING 627 kcals, protein 49g, carbs 44g, fat 30g, sat fat 14g, fibre 5g, sugar 11g, salt 2.13g

Braised lamb shanks

The shanks can be braised up to 2 days ahead, then chilled and reheated in the sauce, or made a month ahead and frozen.

TAKES 1¾ HOURS • SERVES 4

2 tbsp olive oil
4 lamb shanks
1 onion, roughly chopped
2 carrots, roughly chopped
few sprigs rosemary
3 fresh bay leaves
4 garlic cloves, left whole
2 tbsp plain flour
1 tbsp tomato purée
350ml/12fl oz white wine
350ml/12fl lamb or chicken stock
green veg, to serve

1 Heat the oil in a pressure cooker and cook the lamb for about 10 minutes until browned all over. Remove the lamb to a plate, add the onion and carrots, and cook for 10 minutes until starting to brown. Stir in the herbs and garlic, and cook for a few minutes more. Stir in the flour and tomato purée, season well then pour over the wine and stock. Bring to a simmer and submerge the lamb in the sauce. Close the lid, bring up to high pressure and cook for 45 minutes then release the pressure slowly.

2 Remove the lamb from the sauce to a plate. Put the pan back on the heat and bubble the sauce down for about 15 minutes until rich and glossy. Pass it through a sieve into a jug. To serve, reheat the lamb in the sauce, adding a splash of water if the sauce is too thick; serve with green veg alongside.

PER SERVING 712 kcals, protein 67g, carbs 18g, fat 34g, sat fat 12g, fibre 2g, sugar 9g, salt 0.4g

Moroccan meatball tagine with lemon & olives

This dish is wonderfully aromatic. It works well for a dinner party, served with fluffy couscous, or it can also be simply served with crusty bread.

TAKES 50 MINUTES • SERVES 4

3 onions, peeled
500g/1lb 2oz minced lamb
zest and juice 1 unwaxed lemon, plus
    1 whole unwaxed lemon, quartered
1 tsp ground cumin
1 tsp ground cinnamon
pinch cayenne pepper
small bunch flat-leaf parsley, chopped
2 tbsp olive oil
thumb-sized piece ginger, peeled and
    grated
1 red chilli, deseeded and finely
    chopped
pinch saffron strands
250ml/9fl oz lamb stock
1 tbsp tomato purée
100g/4oz pitted black Kalamata olives
small bunch coriander, chopped
couscous or crusty bread, to serve

1 Put the onions in a food processor and blitz until finely chopped. Put the lamb, lemon zest, spices, parsley and half the onions in a large bowl, and season. Using your hands, mix until well combined, then shape into walnut-sized balls.
2 Heat the oil in a pressure cooker then add the remaining onions, the ginger, chilli and saffron. Cook for 5 minutes until the onion is softened and starting to colour. Add the lemon juice, stock, tomato purée and olives, then bring to the boil and add the meatballs. Close the lid, bring up to low pressure and cook for 10 minutes then release the pressure slowly.
3 Add the coriander and lemon wedges, tucking them in among the meatballs. Cook for a further 5–10 minutes, uncovered, until the liquid has reduced and thickened slightly. Serve hot with couscous or crusty bread.

PER SERVING 394 kcals, protein 31g, carbs 11g, fat 26g, sat fat 9g, fibre 3g, sugar 8g, salt 1.7g

Asian aubergine & pork hotpot

Pressure-cooked aubergines become so soft and absorb all the flavour of the stew juices.

TAKES 50 MINUTES • SERVES 4

3 tbsp sunflower oil

750g/1lb 10oz fatty pork, such as shoulder or skinless belly, cut into large chunks

2 aubergines, cut into large chunks

2 tbsp dark muscovado sugar

5 star anise

1 cinnamon stick

2 onions, chopped

large piece ginger, peeled and finely sliced

1 red chilli, deseeded and sliced

1 bunch coriander, leaves and stalks separated, stalks finely chopped

2 tbsp Thai fish sauce, plus extra to taste

juice 1 large lime

1 Heat 2 tablespoons of the oil in a pressure cooker and brown the meat – you may have to do this in batches – then remove to a dish. Add the rest of the oil and the aubergines, brown on all sides, scoop out and add to the pork. Tip the sugar into the pan and leave to caramelise slightly. Return the pork and aubergine to the pan with the star anise and cinnamon, then coat in the caramel.

2 Add the onions, ginger and half the chilli, and cook for a few minutes with the pork. Add the coriander stalks and splash in the fish sauce and enough water to come a quarter of the way up. Close the lid, cook for 30 minutes on high pressure then release the pressure slowly.

3 Add the lime juice and more fish sauce to taste. Stir through half the coriander leaves and the remaining chilli. Tip into a serving dish and scatter over the rest of the coriander.

PER SERVING 574 kcals, protein 38g, carbs 18g, fat 40g, sat fat 13g, fibre 4g, sugar 15g, salt 1.81g

Crispy Mongolian lamb

Try cooking with a different cut of meat and enjoy a meal for two at a fraction of the cost of going out. If you can't find lamb breast, use a 500g/1lb 2oz piece pork belly.

TAKES 2 HOURS 10 MINUTES
- **SERVES 2**

1 lamb breast (about 750g/1lb 10oz)
thumb-sized piece ginger
2 garlic cloves, crushed
6 tbsp dark soy sauce
1 tbsp Chinese five-spice powder
150ml/¼ pint Shaohsing rice wine
2 tbsp light soft brown sugar

TO SERVE

1 round lettuce, leaves separated
¼ cucumber, cut into matchsticks
3 spring onions, cut into finger-length pieces then shredded

1 Put the lamb in the pressure cooker. Add the remaining ingredients plus enough water just to cover. Close the lid, cook for 50 minutes on high then release the pressure slowly. Allow to cool, still covered in the cooking liquid, with the lid on. You can do this 1–2 days in advance and let the lamb cool in the fridge.
2 When cold, lift the lamb out of the liquid and transfer to a baking sheet. Skim the fat from the liquid and bubble in the pan, until thick and syrupy. Pour into a serving bowl. Heat the grill to medium. Grill the lamb until crisp and hot through.
3 Shred the lamb, discarding most of the fat and all the bones, but keep the nice, crisp skin. You can cut off the skin first and leave it in a hot oven while you shred the rest of the meat. To serve, take everything to the table and eat the lamb rolled up in the lettuce leaves with the cucumber, spring onions and sauce.

PER SERVING 643 kcals, protein 54g, carbs 21g, fat 36g, sat fat 18g, fibre none, sugar 20g, salt 5.3g

Braised pork with prunes

Shoulder is one of the cheapest cuts of pork and is perfectly suited for braising with prunes in a classic stew like this.

TAKES 1¼ HOURS • SERVES 4

1 tbsp olive oil
600g/1lb 5oz pork shoulder, roughly cut into 5cm/2in chunks
small knob butter
1 onion, sliced
1 tbsp plain flour
2 large glasses fruity rose or white wine
300ml/½ pint chicken stock
140g/5oz dried prunes (about 12)
handful parsley leaves, chopped, to serve
pasta, to serve (optional)

1 Heat the olive oil in a pressure cooker and cook the pork for about 10 minutes, turning occasionally, until it is brown all over. You need plenty of space in the pan, so cook in batches if needed. Remove from the pan to a plate. Tip out any burnt bits, then add the butter and cook the onion for 3–5 minutes until softened.

2 Stir in the flour, then return the pork and juices to the pan. Pour over the wine and enough stock to cover the meat. Close the lid, bring up to high pressure and cook for 30 minutes then release the pressure quickly. Tip in the prunes, top up with a bit more stock or water if the meat isn't covered, close the lid again, bring up to high pressure and this time cook for 10 minutes then leave the pressure to release naturally. Serve with pasta and sprinkle with parsley.

PER SERVING 497 kcals, protein 29g, carbs 22g, fat 28g, sat fat 10g, fibre 1g, sugar none, salt 0.54g

Really sticky ribs

This simple tomato-and-honey marinade turns pork ribs into a sticky, barbecuey nibble – a real hit with the kids.

TAKES 45 MINUTES • SERVES 6

400ml/14fl oz tomato passata
2 garlic cloves, crushed
2 tbsp reduced-salt soy sauce
3 tbsp clear honey
1 tbsp Worcestershire sauce
1kg/2lb 4oz small lean pork ribs

1 In a large bowl, mix together the passata, garlic, soy sauce, honey and Worcestershire sauce. Add the pork ribs to the bowl and mix well to coat evenly. Tip the ribs and all the sauce into a pressure cooker.

2 Close the lid, bring up to high pressure and cook for 20 minutes then release the pressure slowly. Scoop the ribs out on to a plate. Put the pan over a medium heat and bubble down to a sticky sauce. Toss the ribs back through the sauce and put in a serving dish. Serve with lots of napkins.

PER SERVING 180 kcals, protein 15g, carbs 11g, fat 7g, sat fat 3g, fibre none, sugar 11g, salt 0.7g

Beef massaman curry

If you can't find massaman curry paste then use Thai red curry paste and add a sprinkling of turmeric to the pan as you cook it off.

TAKES 1 HOUR 20 MINUTES
● **SERVES 4**

400ml can coconut cream
4 tbsp massaman curry paste
600g/1lb 5oz stewing beef steak, cut into large chunks
1 onion, cut into thin wedges
4 kaffir lime leaves, fresh or dried
1 cinnamon stick
1 tbsp tamarind paste
1 tbsp palm or light soft brown sugar
1 tbsp Thai fish sauce
85g/3oz unsalted peanuts, roughly chopped
450g/1lb waxy potatoes, cut into 2.5cm/1in chunks
1 red chilli, deseeded and finely sliced, to garnish
jasmine rice, to serve

1 Heat 2 tablespoons of the coconut cream in a pressure cooker, add the curry paste and fry for 1 minute, then stir in the beef and fry until well coated and sealed. Stir in the rest of the coconut with half a can of water, the onion, lime leaves, cinnamon, tamarind, sugar, fish sauce and most of the peanuts. Close the lid, bring up to high pressure and cook for 40 minutes, then release the pressure quickly.
2 Stir in the potatoes, close the lid, bring up to high pressure again and cook for 5 minutes more, then release the pressure slowly.
3 Tip the beef into a serving dish and sprinkle with sliced chilli and the remaining peanuts, and serve with jasmine rice.

PER SERVING 734 kcals, protein 44g, carbs 38g, fat 46g, sat fat 21g, fibre 3g, sugar 13g, salt 1.87g

Sticky lemon pork

Rice, buttered pasta or boiled new potatoes would all make great accompaniments to this simple stew.

TAKES 55 MINUTES ● SERVES 4

3 tbsp plain flour
1 tbsp paprika
800g/1lb 12oz leg or shoulder of pork, cut into large chunks
2 tbsp olive oil
2 rosemary sprigs, leaves stripped
4 garlic cloves, chopped
2 bay leaves
300ml/½ pint white wine
peeled zest and juice 1 lemon

1 Tip the flour, paprika and some salt and pepper into a food bag and toss the pork in it until coated. Heat the oil in a pressure cooker and fry the pork until brown on all sides. Add the rosemary, garlic and bay, then fry for 1 minute more. Pour in the wine and bring to the boil, scraping the bottom of the pan. Lower to a simmer and throw in the lemon zest.

2 Close the lid, bring up to high pressure and cook for 30 minutes then release the pressure quickly – the pork should now be very tender. Just before serving, stir in the lemon juice and check the seasoning.

PER SERVING 356 kcals, protein 46g, carbs 14g, fat 11g, sat fat 3g, fibre 1g, sugar 4g, salt 0.34g

Braised beef shin with melting onions

Beef shin braises to a melting texture far better than whole braising steaks, which can end up dry, even though they are tender.

TAKES 1 HOUR 40 MINUTES
- **SERVES 4**

4 thick generous slices beef shin (about 700g/1lb 9oz total)

plain flour, for dusting

2 tbsp sunflower oil

3 medium onions, halved and thinly sliced

2 tsp caster sugar

6 garlic cloves, sliced

700ml/1¼ pints beef stock (made with 2 cubes)

3 tbsp Worcestershire sauce

4 large flat mushrooms, thickly sliced

chopped parsley leaves, to garnish

seasonal veg, to serve

1 Dust the beef in the flour. Heat the oil in a pressure cooker. Add the onions and fry for 5 minutes. Add the sugar and cook for 5–10 minutes, stirring frequently, until the onions are caramelised. Stir in the garlic for the final few minutes.

2 Pour in the stock and stir in the Worcestershire sauce. Add the beef and mushrooms, then season, adding plenty of black pepper. Close the lid, bring up to high pressure and cook for 50 minutes then release the pressure slowly. It can all now be chilled for up to 3 days. To freeze, cool and store in freezer bags for up to 3 months, then when defrosted, reheat in a pan. Once piping hot, transfer to a serving dish, scatter with the parsley and serve with seasonal veg.

PER SERVING 364 kcals, protein 44g, carbs 11g, fat 16g, sat fat 5g, fibre 2g, sugar 8g, salt 1.03g

Lemon marmalade

The pressure-cooker method for making marmalade means the lemons are cooked whole then cut up, which is far less time-consuming than cutting them up when raw.

**TAKES 1 HOUR ● MAKES
6 X 450ML JARS**
1kg/2lb 4oz unwaxed lemons
2kg/4lb 8oz granulated sugar

1 Chill a saucer. Wash the lemons and remove the top 'button'. Put in a pressure cooker with 1.5 litres/2½ pints water. Close the lid cook for 15 minutes on high then reduce the pressure slowly.

2 Remove the lemons from the pan once cool. You'll need 1.5 litres/2½ pints in total. If you don't quite have this, make up the difference with water.

3 Halve the lemons, remove and reserve the pips and any juice. Cut the lemon peel and flesh into strips. Then put all of this back into the pan. Put the pips in a small piece of muslin and tie up then add to the pan. Add the sugar and bring to the boil, stirring until dissolved. Boil rapidly for about 20 minutes until setting point is reached. This is when a little marmalade dropped on to the chilled saucer, then cooled, crinkles when pushed gently.

4 Leave to cool for 10 minutes, then remove the muslin. Pour into warm sterilised jars and seal straight away.

PER SERVING (15g) 40 kcals, protein none, carbs 10g, fat none, sat fat none, fibre none, sugar 10g, salt none

Fragrant mango & apple chutney

This homemade chutney makes a lovely gift for a friend, but keep some for yourself to have with cheese or cold meats.

TAKES 1½ HOURS ● MAKES ABOUT 4 x 500ML JARS

3 large ripe mangoes (about 1kg/2¼lb total)
2 tbsp sunflower oil
2 onions, halved and thinly sliced
thumb-sized piece ginger, peeled and cut into thin shreds
10 green cardamom pods
1 cinnamon stick
½ tsp cumin seeds
½ tsp coriander seeds, lightly crushed
¼ tsp black onion seeds (nigella or kalonji)
½ tsp turmeric powder
2 Bramley apples (about 500g/1lb 2oz total), peeled, cored and chopped
1 large red chilli, deseeded and finely chopped
375ml/13fl oz white wine vinegar
400g/14oz golden caster sugar

1 Cut each mango in half. Cut the flesh of each half into chunky diagonal pieces – take care not to cut through the skin. Turn each half inside out, then slice away the chunks of mango that stand proud. Cut the flesh from around the stones, trim off the skin and chop the flesh.

2 Heat the oil in a pressure cooker, add the onions and fry until soft. Stir in the ginger and cook, stirring, until the onion is golden. Stir in the spices, except the turmeric, and fry until toasted.

3 Stir in the turmeric, then add the apple, mango and chilli, and pour in 500ml/ 18fl oz water. Close the lid, cook for 12 minutes on high then fast-release the pressure.

4 Remove the lid, pour in the vinegar, stir in the sugar and 1 teaspoon salt, then simmer, uncovered, for 30 minutes, stirring frequently until the mixture is pulpy. Spoon into sterilised jars.

PER TBSP 17 kcals, protein none, carbs 4g, fat none, sat fat none, fibre none, sugar 4g, salt none

Summer berry jam

Remember to chill a saucer in plenty of time for that all-important setting test. The jam will then keep in a cool, dark place for at least 6 months.

TAKES 1¼ HOURS • MAKES ROUGHLY 1 LITRE/1¾ PINTS, ABOUT 2 X 450ML JARS

900g/2lb mixed summer berries (I used hulled strawberries – large ones halved – raspberries, redcurrants, blackcurrants and a few early blackberries)

750kg/1lb 10oz jam sugar (the one with added pectin)

juice and pips 1 lemon

small knob butter (optional)

1 Before you start, put a small saucer in the freezer. Tip the berries into a pressure cooker with the sugar and use a potato masher to mash the two together to release all the juices. Give it all a good stir to start the sugar dissolving. Stir in the lemon juice, then collect all the pips and secure them inside a tea strainer or piece of muslin before adding to the pan too.

2 Close the lid and cook for 3 minutes on high then release the pressure slowly. Remove the lid and bring back to the boil until the mixture reaches 105C/221F on a cooking thermometer or until a little hot jam poured on to a chilled saucer wrinkles when pushed with your finger.

3 Skim off any excess scum then stir in the knob of butter, if you want – this will help to dissolve any remaining scum. Leave the jam for 15 minutes before ladling into sterilised jars. Refrigerate jars once opened.

PER TBSP 44 kcals, protein none, carbs 12g, fat none, sat fat none, fibre none, sugar 12g, salt none

Winter spice jelly

This delicious jelly brings a welcome touch of sharpness and spice to your plate and works really well with any meaty leftovers.

TAKES 3 HOURS, PLUS SETTING

● **MAKES 2 JARS**

FOR THE JELLY

1kg/2lb 4oz cooking apples
2 cinnamon sticks
2 star anise
11 cloves
½ nutmeg, grated
4 allspice berries
1 blade mace or ¼ tsp ground mace
4 long pieces orange peel
6 bay leaves
450g/1lb jam sugar
100ml/3½fl oz cider vinegar

FOR THE JARS

2 star anise
4 whole cloves
2 bay leaves

1 Cut the apples into small chunks, leaving the peel and cores in. Tip the apple into a pressure cooker with the spices, orange peel and bay leaves. Cover with 400ml/14fl oz water, close the lid, cook for 5 minutes on high then reduce the pressure slowly. Mash the contents a few times.

2 Pour the apple mixture into a sieve lined with muslin or a J-cloth, suspended over a large bowl. Leave undisturbed until it stops dripping for 2 hours or overnight.

3 Measure the juice – you need 600ml/1 pint. Pour into the cleaned pressure cooker with the jam sugar and vinegar.

4 Set over a low heat to dissolve the sugar, stirring. Bring to the boil and boil rapidly for 15 minutes, skimming away any scum that rises to the surface.

5 Pour the jelly into hot sterilised jars and put a star anise, bay leaf and 2 cloves into each jar. Chill for 3–4 hours until set.

PER TBSP 125 kcals, protein none, carbs 33g, fat none, sat fat none, fibre none, sugar 33g, salt 0.01g

Winter fruit compote

A healthy pud that's just as tasty eaten cold for breakfast the following day.

TAKES 40 MINUTES • SERVES 4

500g pack mixed dried fruit
200ml/7fl oz fresh orange juice
½ cinnamon stick
6 whole cloves
6 black peppercorns
0% Greek yogurt or low-fat fromage
    frais, to serve

1 Tip the dried fruit, orange juice and whole spices into a pressure cooker. Close the lid, bring up to high pressure and cook for 3 minutes then reduce the pressure slowly. Remove the lid, stir and put back on the heat until the juices become sticky and the fruits are plump.
2 Leave the compote to stand for a minute and serve in bowls with spoonfuls of yogurt or fromage frais.

PER SERVING 352 kcals, protein 3g, carbs 89g, fat 1g, sat fat none, fibre 3g, sugar none, salt 0.15g

Steamed vanilla sponge with butterscotch sauce & custard

There couldn't be a better way to end a weekend meal than with this indulgent pud.

TAKES 1 HOUR ● **SERVES 4**

FOR THE SPONGE

250g/9oz butter, softened, plus extra
   for greasing
250g/9oz caster sugar
4 eggs
1 tsp vanilla extract
250g/9oz plain flour
1 tsp baking powder
50ml/2fl oz milk
custard, to serve

FOR THE BUTTERSCOTCH SAUCE

75g/2½oz caster sugar
25g/1oz butter
50ml/2fl oz double cream

1 Butter a 1.5-litre pudding basin. Cream the butter and sugar in a mixing bowl until pale and fluffy. Add the eggs one at a time, mixing well, then add the vanilla.

2 Sift the flour and baking powder into the bowl and fold into the sponge mixture until smooth. Stir in the milk.

3 Fill the basin with the mixture and cover with a double layer of buttered foil and baking parchment, making a pleat in the centre. Tie the foil securely with string then place in a steamer. Put on the trivet of a pressure cooker and pour in 500ml boiling water. Cover with lid, not to pressure, and steam for 15 minutes. Close the lid and steam for 25 minutes on high then slow-release the pressure.

4 On a low heat dissolve the sugar with 2 tbsp water. Bring to the boil; do not stir. Once a caramel has formed, whisk in the butter. Stir in the cream off the heat. To serve, turn out the sponge, drizzle with the sauce and serve with the custard.

PER SERVING 308 kcals, protein 18g, carbs 148g, fat 75g, sat fat 43g, fibre 2g, sugar 98g, salt 1.5g

Poached pears in spiced red wine

The pears in this fat-free dessert really take on the flavours of the spices and thyme, and become beautifully coloured by the red wine.

TAKES 20 MINUTES • SERVES 6

1 vanilla pod
750ml red wine
225g/8oz caster sugar
1 cinnamon stick, halved
1 thyme sprig, plus extra to decorate
6 pears, peeled, but kept whole with
    stalk intact

1 Halve the vanilla pod lengthways, scrape out the black seeds, reserving the pod, and put the seeds in a pressure cooker with the wine, sugar, cinnamon and thyme. Cut each piece of pod into three long, thin strips, add to the pan, then lower in the pears.

2 Close the lid, bring up to high pressure and cook the pears for 6 minutes then release the pressure quickly. The cooking time will depend on the ripeness of your pears – they should be tender all the way through when pierced with a cocktail stick; if not, cook for 2 minutes more. You can make these up to 2 days ahead and chill.

3 Take the pears from the pan, then boil the liquid to reduce it by half so that it's syrupy. Serve each pear with the cooled syrup, a strip of vanilla, a piece of cinnamon and a small thyme sprig.

PER SERVING 235 kcals, protein none, carbs 51g, fat none, sat fat none, fibre 2g, sugar 51g, salt 0.3g

A nice rice pudding

Here's a basic recipe for pressure-cooker rice pudding – add other flavours such as lemon or orange zest, vanilla or cinnamon.

TAKES 30 MINUTES ● SERVES 4

25g/1oz butter
100g/4oz pudding rice
50g/2oz sugar
700ml/1¼ pint milk
pinch grated nutmeg

1 Melt the butter in a pressure cooker, then tip in the rice and sugar, stir through the milk and bring to a simmer. Close the lid, bring up to high pressure and cook for 12 minutes then release the pressure slowly.
2 Remove the lid, sprinkle with nutmeg, stir well, return to the heat for 1–2 minutes and simmer to thicken. Spoon into dishes to serve.

PER SERVING 214 kcals, protein 8g, carbs 40g, fat 3g, sat fat 2g, fibre none, sugar 21g, salt 0.19g

Schooldays treacle sponge

This updated version of a retro pud is lighter but still has all the charm of syrupy sponge and sticky sauce.

TAKES 1½ HOURS • SERVES 4 GENEROUSLY

175g/6oz unsalted butter, softened, plus extra for greasing
3 tbsp golden syrup, plus extra for drizzling (optional)
1 tbsp fresh white breadcrumbs
splash brandy (optional but delicious)
175g/6oz golden caster sugar
zest 1 lemon
3 eggs, beaten
175g/6oz self-raising flour
2 tbsp milk
clotted cream, to serve

1 Use a small knob of butter heavily to grease a 1-litre pudding basin. In a small bowl, mix the golden syrup with the breadcrumbs and brandy, if using, then tip into the pudding basin.

2 Beat the butter with the sugar and zest until light and fluffy, then add the eggs. Fold in the flour, then add the milk.

3 Spoon the mix into the pudding basin. Cover with a double layer of buttered foil and baking paper, making a pleat in the centre to allow the pudding to rise. Tie the foil securely with string, then put on the trivet of a pressure cooker and pour in 500ml/18fl oz kettle-hot water. Cover with the lid, not to pressure but just to steam the pudding for 15 minutes. Close the lid, bring up to high pressure and steam for 35 minutes then release the pressure slowly. Turn out on to a serving dish. Serve with lashings of clotted cream and a little extra golden syrup drizzled over, if you want.

PER SERVING 763 kcals, protein 10g, carbs 90g, fat 43g, sat fat 25g, fibre 1g, sugar 56g, salt 0.71g

Vanilla-poached peaches

Ripe peaches are poached to perfection in this light, honeyed syrup. Great with shortbread or other buttery biscuits.

TAKES 30 MINUTES ● SERVES 4

4 large ripe peaches
425ml/¾ pint sweet white wine
2 tbsp clear honey
1 vanilla pod, split
clotted cream, to serve (optional)

1 Put the kettle on and fill a large bowl with iced water. Put the peaches in another large bowl and pour over enough boiling water to cover. Leave for 30 seconds, then remove the peaches with a slotted spoon and plunge them into the cold water. The skins should now peel away easily.

2 Put the wine, honey and vanilla pod in a pressure cooker, and gently heat until the honey has dissolved. Lower in the peaches, close the lid, cook for 5 minutes on low then release the pressure quickly. Remove the cooked peaches from the pan and set to one side in a large bowl.

3 Boil the syrup hard until it has reduced by half (this will take about 10 minutes). Spoon over the peaches, then set aside to cool. The peaches will keep for up to 2 days, covered and in the fridge. Serve the peaches and syrup at room temperature, warm or chilled with spoonfuls of clotted cream, if you like.

PER SERVING 162 kcals, protein 1g, carbs 21g, fat trace, sat fat none, fibre 20g, sugar 6g, salt trace

Sticky date & raisin pudding

An irresistible dessert that combines all the best bits of a sticky toffee pudding and a classic steamed sponge. Serve with a caramel sauce.

TAKES 1 HOUR 20 MINUTES
● **SERVES 8**

250g/9oz stoned dates, roughly chopped
100g/4oz raisins
150ml/¼ pint milk
150ml/¼ pint brandy or rum
140g/5oz butter, softened, plus extra for greasing
50g/2oz soft brown sugar
2 eggs
175g/6oz self-raising flour
1 tsp ground mixed spice
zest 1 orange

1 Put the dates, raisins, milk and brandy or rum in a small pan, bring to the boil and simmer for 5 minutes then cool. Butter a 1.2-litre pudding basin.
2 Cut a circle of baking parchment and one of foil, both 5cm/2in wider than the rim of your pudding basin. Make a pleat down the centre of both, then butter one side of the parchment.
3 Beat the butter and sugar until pale. Add the eggs and beat until combined. Add the flour, mixed spice, orange zest, a pinch of salt and the date mixture, and stir until smooth. Tip into the basin. Cover with the parchment, butter-side down, then the foil. Tie with string under the lip.
4 Stand the pudding basin on the trivet of a pressure cooker and pour in 500ml/ 18fl oz boiling water. Cover with the lid, not to pressure. Steam the pudding for 15 minutes. Close the lid, bring up to high, steam for 35 minutes then release the pressure slowly. Turn out on to a dish.

PER SERVING 418 kcals, protein 6g, carbs 50g, fat 17g, sat fat 10g, fibre 3g, sugar 36g, salt 0.6g

Spotted Dick

Steam a traditional fruity sponge pudding made with suet, citrus zest and currants then serve in thick slices with hot custard.

TAKES 1¼ HOURS • SERVES 4

200g/7oz self-raising flour
100g/4oz shredded suet
140g/5oz currants
75g/2½oz caster sugar
finely grated zest 1 lemon and 1 small
    orange
100ml/3½fl oz whole milk, plus
    2–3 tbsp (optional)
hot custard, to serve

1 Put the flour and a pinch of salt in a bowl. Add the suet, currants, sugar, lemon and orange zest. Pour in the milk and mix to a firm but moist dough, adding the extra milk if necessary.
2 Shape into a fat roll about 15cm/6in long or shorter to fit in your pressure cooker. Put on a large rectangle of baking parchment. Wrap loosely to allow for the pudding to rise and tie the ends with string like a Christmas cracker.
3 Set up the steamer trivet in a pressure cooker and add 500ml/18fl oz boiling water from the kettle then add the pudding. Cover, not for pressure but to steam for 20 minutes then close the lid, bring up to low pressure and continue to cook for 25 minutes, then reduce the pressure slowly. Remove the pudding from the steamer and allow to cool slightly before unwrapping. Serve sliced with hot custard.

PER SERVING 561 kcals, protein 6g, carbs 80g, fat 24g, sat fat 13g, fibre 2g, sugar 43g, salt 0.6g

Heavenly chocolate pudding

A foolproof recipe for an indulgent, fudgy chocolate pudding, with an extra hit of chocolate from a rich sauce.

TAKES 1 HOUR 20 MINUTES

● **SERVES 6**

100g/4oz butter, plus extra for greasing
2 tbsp golden syrup
100g/4oz dark muscovado sugar
150ml/¼ pint milk
1 egg (large or medium)
1 heaped tbsp cocoa powder
225g/8oz self-raising flour, minus
   1 heaped tbsp
1 tsp ground cinnamon
¼ tsp bicarbonate of soda

FOR THE CHOCOLATE SAUCE

4 tbsp milk
4 tbsp cream
1 tbsp golden syrup
100g/4oz good-quality dark chocolate

1 Butter the inside of a 1.2-litre pudding bowl and line the base with a disc of buttered greaseproof paper.

2 Melt the butter, syrup and sugar in a pan. Remove from the heat and stir in the milk and egg. Add the cocoa to the flour, then tip this mixture into the pan with the cinnamon and soda.

3 Pour the mixture into the pudding bowl and cover tightly with foil. Put the pudding on the trivet of a pressure cooker and pour in 500ml/18fl oz kettle-hot water. Cover with the lid, not to pressure but to steam the pudding for 15 minutes. Close the lid, bring up to high pressure and steam for 30 minutes then release the pressure slowly. Meanwhile, heat the sauce ingredients until melted, stirring all the time.

4 Turn the pudding out (run a knife around the inside of the bowl, if necessary) and discard the paper disc. Pour the sauce over the top and serve.

PER SERVING 472 kcals, protein 4g, carbs 50g, fat 30g, sat fat 14g, fibre 3g, sugar 29g, salt 0.9g

Christmas pudding with citrus & spice

Although you can buy excellent Christmas puddings, this fruity version is worth the effort and using a pressure cooker cuts down the cooking time.

TAKES 2½ HOURS, PLUS OVERNIGHT SOAKING • SERVES 10

175g/6oz each raisins, currants and sultanas
140g/5oz whole glacé cherries
50g/2oz chopped mixed peel
50g/2oz whole blanched almonds
zest 1 orange and 1 lemon
1 medium carrot, peeled and finely grated
150ml/¼ pint brandy
50ml/2fl oz orange liqueur, such as Grand Marnier
175g/6oz light muscovado sugar
175g/6oz fresh white breadcrumbs
125g/4½oz self-raising flour
1 tsp ground mixed spice
¼ tsp grated nutmeg
175g/6oz butter, frozen, plus extra butter for greasing
2 eggs, beaten
extra-thick double cream or vanilla ice cream, to serve
sprig holly, to decorate

1 Mix the fruit, almonds, citrus, carrot, brandy and orange liqueur in a large bowl. Cover and leave overnight.

2 Mix all the dry ingredients, then add to the soaked-fruit mixture. Grate in the butter, then add the eggs and stir.

3 Grease a 1.5-litre pudding basin and line the base with greaseproof paper. Spoon in the mixture and cover the surface with a round of greaseproof paper, then cover the basin with foil and double-thickness greaseproof paper and tie at the rim with string. Put the pudding on the trivet of a pressure cooker and pour in 1 litre/1¾ pints kettle-hot water. Cover with the lid, not to pressure. Steam for 15 minutes. Close the lid, steam for 1¾ hours on high then release the pressure slowly.

4 Cool, then store for up to a year. When ready to serve, set up the pressure cooker as before but close the lid, bring to high, cook for 15 minutes, then release the pressure slowly. Decorate with holly.

PER SERVING 596 kcals, protein 7g, carbs 92g, fat 20g, sat fat 10g, fibre 3g, sugar 69g, salt 0.89g

Index

Also available from BBC Books and *Good Food*